Also by Gary Hart

The Shield and the Cloak:
The Security of the Commons

God and Caesar in America:
An Essay on Religion and Politics

James Monroe
(The American Presidents Series)

The Fourth Power:
A New Grand Strategy for the United States in the Twenty-first Century

Restoration of the Republic:
The Jeffersonian Ideal in 21st-Century America

The Minuteman:
Restoring an Army of the People

The Patriot:
An Exhortation to Liberate America from the Barbarians

The Good Fight:
The Education of an American Reformer

Russia Shakes the World:
The Second Russian Revolution and Its Impact on the World

The New Democracy

The Strategies of Zeus

America Can Win:
The Case for Military Reform (with William S. Lind)

The Double Man
(with William S. Cohen)

Right from the Start:
A Chronicle of the McGovern Campaign

THE COURAGE OF
OUR CONVICTIONS

THE **COURAGE** OF OUR **CONVICTIONS**

A MANIFESTO FOR **DEMOCRATS**

GARY HART ★ ★ ★

TIMES BOOKS | HENRY HOLT AND COMPANY | NEW YORK

Times Books
Henry Holt and Company, LLC
Publishers since 1866
175 Fifth Avenue
New York, New York 10010
www.henryholt.com

Distributed in Canada by H. B. Fenn and Company Ltd.

Library of Congress Cataloging-in-Publication Data

Hart, Gary, 1936–
  The courage of our convictions : a manifesto for Democrats /
Gary Hart.—1st ed.
      p. cm.
  ISBN-13: 978-0-8050-8662-1
  ISBN-10: 0-8050-8662-5
  1. Democratic Party (U.S.)   2. United States—Politics
and government—2001–   I. Title.

JK2316.H38 2006
324.2736—dc22

                                        2006044490

First Edition 2006

Designed by Victoria Hartman

Printed in the United States of America

P1

This book is in acknowledgment
and, in too many cases, in memory of:

Mike Mansfield, for his statesmanship
Philip Hart, for his integrity
George McGovern and Eugene McCarthy,
    for their courage
Gaylord Nelson, for his wisdom
Hubert Humphrey, for his humanity
Abe Ribicoff, for his diplomacy and
Ed Muskie, Frank Church, Ted Kennedy,

and a number of others like them,
who represent and represented
conviction and courage
in keeping the flame and promise
of the Democratic Party alive

Here I am,
the old dog for the hard road.

—Seamus Heaney,
The Burial at Thebes

CONTENTS

Contents

THE COURAGE OF
OUR CONVICTIONS

INTRODUCTION

"The best lack all conviction," Yeats might well have written for today, "while the worst are full of passionate intensity." That passionate intensity, always so near the crusader's soul, is a far different thing from genuine conviction rooted in principle, history, and moral purpose. Though there is often a fine line between them, in that difference rests the integrity of a democratic republic.

Like pride, conviction is one of those rare qualities resisting excess. It is possible to have either too much or too little of both. In the mind of the dictator, too much conviction is the source of tyranny. In the mind of the democrat, too little conviction is the source of drift and calculation.

Courage may be defined as a beneficent act against self-interest—risking one's life for another; risking one's career for a principle; taking an unpopular stand, particularly against powerful interests; saying what needs to be said when others remain silent. It means standing for something larger than oneself and one's own interests. America's founders complimented those who were "disinterested." Then, the disinterested citizen was one who placed the common good, the collective interest, above his or her own interest. Today we confuse being disinterested with being uninterested.

In the political arena the enemies of courage are calculation and careerism. The warmest friend of courage is conviction based on principle. Conviction requires a moral base and compass, for the world's worst scoundrels often proclaim the strongest conviction.

This is a meditation, perhaps a long essay, a series of connected short essays, or even a sermon, on the themes of courage and conviction, especially as they are required now for a twenty-first-century Democratic Party renaissance. In the fall of 2005, I was shocked to be told by a Democratic United States senator that the Democratic caucus in the Senate was going to take up the question "What do we stand for?" In the Senate of the 1970s, in which I served, such a question would never have occurred to us. We all knew what we stood for, and there was remarkable unanimity on many issues.

What has happened? Why do people in small towns, in large cities, and on college campuses ask, "What do the Democrats stand for? Why are the party leaders so quiet?"

These questions have become more frequent and more intense as the war in Iraq drags on into its fourth year with no resolution in sight and no definition by President George W. Bush of the "course" we are to "stay." Yet Democratic leaders, including most of those preparing to seek the presidency in 2008, and especially those who voted for the war resolution in October 2002, find protection and anonymity in silence.

What do we stand for, indeed? It has become painfully apparent that the great Democratic Party, the dominant party of the twentieth century, the party that led America through two world wars and much of the Cold War, has become mute. The best Democrats lack all conviction, or at least all courage to state what those convictions are, while the worst conservatives, those full of passionate intensity, fill the vacuum in governance.

This book seeks to explore when, where, why, and how the Democratic Party lost its way—and its courage. But it also proposes a manifesto for the future, a manifesto constructed of the best of our twentieth-century heritage, a manifesto based upon the legacy of Franklin D. Roosevelt, Harry S. Truman, John F. Kennedy, and Lyndon B. Johnson. Without that heritage and legacy there would have been no Carter or Clinton presidencies. And without that heritage and legacy there will be no Democratic presidencies or Congresses anytime soon.

Finally, I challenge all in my party, the Democratic Party, who dispute the manifesto proposed here, or the roots from which it springs, to state as specifically and concretely as possible what *they* believe the Democratic Party stands for and why they believe it deserves to lead our nation once again.

The purpose here is not to propound a declaration but rather to stimulate debate and reflection. At its best the Democratic presidential nomination process leading to the national election in 2008 can and should be a debate over the party's core beliefs and purposes. If the next presidential race devolves, as it traditionally does, into a mere contest for money, interest group endorsements, transient poll numbers, media advisers, press courtship, and commercial television advertising, then it will excite no broader interest than among full-time political activists, and it will leave the American people still in grave doubt over who the Democrats really are.

But if the 2008 contest for party leadership should become the occasion for a serious discussion about the Democratic Party's core beliefs and principles, and the policies those principles dictate, then it will be the occasion for restoration of the party and the proof of our qualification for national leadership.

Political parties must continually justify their existence. They do so not merely by the policies they propose but more significantly by the principles they stand for. It is not an easy thing for the Democratic Party, a coalition political party, to identify and coalesce around agreed principles. But once it forces itself through the difficult process of self-examination and self-definition, it is in much better condition to present itself to the public at large as the institution prepared to guide the nation forward.

That self-definition has not taken place since the end of the New Deal era in the late 1960s. Indeed, if anything, the Democratic Party has become more diffuse, more ill-defined, and more confusing to the American people.

In an age of ego, celebrity, and personality, there has been an overpowering search for a leader on a white horse, an exciting new candidate who will lead the Democratic Party out of the wilderness. This search has become a substitute for thought, for purpose, for conviction. Twenty-first-century Democrats cling to the hope of a messiah in the vacant centrist venue where messiahs never appear.

Instead, the Democratic Party must decide what its core principles are and then, and only then, decide which national leader or leaders best embody those principles. No politician can save a political party that does not know what it stands for.

It is well beyond the scope of this book to propose detailed domestic and foreign policies. The author's efforts to provide policy "beef," for those who appreciate the reference, are contained in a number of previous works.* This

---

*See the author's *Restoration of the Republic: The Jeffersonian Ideal in 21st-Century America* (Oxford University Press, 2002), *The Fourth Power: A New Grand Strategy for the United States in the Twenty-first Century* (Oxford University Press, 2004), *The Shield and the Cloak: The Security of the Commons* (Oxford University Press, 2006), and a variety of other books and articles.

present effort is directed rather at reconstituting a governing manifesto from the rich Democratic heritage and culture of the previous century and seeking to apply its principles to the new realities of the twenty-first century, a century of international integration, failed states, information tsunamis, and urban warfare.

This base of Democratic conviction must be the foundation for the courageous promotion of a renewed internationalism founded on new international institutions and alliances, the restoration of principles of equality and social justice at home, and the reminder essential to all republics that we must earn our rights by performance of our duties.

It is our duty to our nation to prove that the best have not lost all conviction.

PART ONE

THE CRISIS
OF THE
DEMOCRATIC
PARTY

1

PROFILES IN CAUTION
AND CALCULATION

The spring and summer of 2002 will eventually come to be seen as a critical moment in our history. For it was during these months that decisions were made, first in the White House, then ratified in the fall by Congress, to undertake an imperial policy in the Middle East in the name of the "war on terrorism."

It would require the loss of more than twenty-five hundred American military personnel, the wounding of almost twenty thousand others, and the death of fifty thousand Iraqis before the fallacies and misleading assertions underlying the logic of the war finally began to be revealed. By then, the United States found itself in the historically uncharacteristic position of an occupying power in a volatile land, in an even more volatile region, that it had preemptively and unnecessarily invaded. By the spring of 2006, two-thirds of the American people, including millions who had trustingly supported the invasion as an action necessary to protect the United States and their families from terrorists, concluded that the enterprise was questionable at least and badly misconceived at best.

Having now produced more history in the early twenty-first century than it is likely to consume for a very long time, the United States (and the many historians sifting through the convoluted foreign policy of this time) may contemplate at considerable leisure, and possibly come to repent, what it wrought. This broad canvas, and a particularly ugly one at that, must be left for others, in other forums, to fill with color. What concerns us here are the reasons why many in the Democratic Party, including many of its national figures in both houses of Congress, surrendered so supinely to an undertaking deeply questionable in its premises and fatally flawed in its conclusions with so little challenge, with such superficial justification, and so completely contrary to America's history, character, and principles.

How did this happen? Why were more questions not asked and more answers demanded? In addition to figures such as Edward Kennedy, Robert C. Byrd, Russell Feingold, and Bob Graham, why did not more party leaders, potential and actual candidates for the presidency especially, take to the floor of the House and Senate on a daily basis to raise doubts, to surface suspicions, *to ask questions*? The response from the Democratic leaders was that all the questions were being answered by the president and vice president, by a respected secretary of state (with the director of Central Intelligence peering knowingly over his shoulder at the United Nations), by an experienced secretary of defense who had access to the best intelligence in the world, and by a forceful and articulate national security adviser who possessed unlimited access to the president. "What further questions could possibly have been asked?" defensive prowar Democrats might and did respond.

Let us suggest at least four questions that a Denver lawyer with no access to the (phony) classified briefings did ask repeatedly in speeches around the country from late summer 2002 until the troops crossed the Iraqi border on March 20, 2003, when such questions became academic:

- What other nations are going with us?
- How long will we be there?
- How much will it cost?
- What are the estimated American casualties?

These questions were then, and are still today, dismissed as either unanswerable, irrelevant, or at the very least silly and impertinent. The small handful of citizen Jeremiahs were lectured: "Remember, we are in a war against terrorism." Presumably this also meant, by implication, "And in wartime, keep your mouth shut and support the president."

Let's think about that. Regarding the first question, administration and Pentagon spokespersons continue to refer to "coalition forces" in Iraq. This is a fiction. With the exception of four British battalions—roughly eight thousand troops, many of whom are in combat support roles—this is and always has been an American enterprise. Chanting "coalition forces" over and over again does not make the prolonged Iraqi occupation any kind of genuine coalition undertaking.

The only arena in which our allies participated in meaningful numbers was as targets of retaliation. In the summer of 2005, London's subways and buses were bombed, in a Britain whose public was seriously at odds with its prime minister over Iraq. This followed by a year the bombing of four trains in Madrid; the Spanish government, which had supplied token forces in Iraq, was turned out of office within days. Nevertheless, in the eyes of history and the world this is an American war, and it is America that will suffer overwhelmingly the military, political, and economic consequences. If there is any doubt about this, ask yourself this question: Were there any "coalition" allies on the deck of the aircraft carrier when George W. Bush gave his famous "Mission Accomplished" performance?

The failure of the Bush administration to convince our traditional allies, principally the western European democracies with whom we had won two world wars and the Cold War, was well known in the run-up to the Iraq invasion.

Many of our allies believed, with some evidence, that our secretary of state's testimony before the United Nations was prepared by the Brothers Grimm. Rather than deal seriously with the objections, questions, and concerns of these traditional allies and the rest of the world community, the American administration and its many media supporters chose rather to mock dissenters as weak, vacillating, and spineless— and to single out the French particularly for being, in the contemptuous phrase popular among supporters of the Bush administration, "cheese-eating surrender monkeys." (Contrary to popular history, ninety thousand French soldiers died in the vain defense of their country against the six weeks' German blitzkrieg in 1940, primarily because their military leaders were still prepared for the previous world war. The easy contempt shown by Bush administration officials toward France verifies that they learned little from that history.)

Had our government been less arrogant and more concerned with maintaining our traditional alliances, it might have listened to the doubts and questions being raised much more seriously and insightfully from foreign democratic capitals than from the cautious "opposition" Democratic Party in the United States. So, to answer the first question—*what other nations are going with us?*—instead of prattling on about "coalition forces," honest leadership would have replied, "Though the British are playing a relatively small supporting role, this is pretty much an American operation."

How long will we be there? Much of the Democratic leadership blithely accepted the assumption put forward by the Bush administration that the invasion would be a walkover and the occupation a great picnic on the lawns of Baghdad with Iraqi children putting flowers in American rifle barrels. Some did ask, "What if . . . ?" But these questions were crushed like flies to wanton boys.

Democratic insistence, supported by a less acquiescent press, in asking the "what if" question might possibly have forced an arrogant administration to address the potential of long-term occupation, a possibility assiduously resisted by the Bush neoconservatives. Why think about it at all when our reliable source and highly paid retainer, Ahmed Chalabi, promised it would never happen, that the Iraqi public all the way up to the doors of the Saddam Hussein household would embrace democracy—and us—with the warmth and intensity reserved for the great liberators of history?

For if even a remote possibility of resistance, insurgency, and long-term occupation were to be admitted, that would have changed everything. Attention and resources would have to be redirected away from the genuine war on terrorism in Afghanistan; the cost to the taxpayer would not only soar, it would be virtually limitless; we could well see thousands of Americans dead and tens of thousands wounded; we might embitter the very people we came to democratize; we might further destabilize an already unstable Middle East region and wider Arab world; we might drive an even deeper wedge between ourselves and the international community. Given these disastrous possibilities, better to assume the best, operate from this blissful assumption, and thus not contemplate, let alone discuss with the American people, less-than-rosy scenarios.

Besides, all this occurred in an age when the ultimate default position, "stay the course," could be widely mistaken for genuine policy.

Now that this very nightmare scenario has come to pass, and we now confront all these extremely ugly realities, the American people rightly ask, "Why weren't we told that even a slight possibility existed that we could end up assuming the British imperial role of a half century before?" "Why was this possibility not considered and planned for?" "Why was it not openly and honestly discussed?" "Were our superconfident leaders so swept up in the arrogance of power that they could entertain no doubt of their ability to dictate terms and dominate Iraqi behavior?" Most of all, "Where was the opposition party, where were the Democrats on whom the nation depended to ask the difficult and penetrating questions?" Where, indeed.

How much will it cost? Of course, the costs of the war in terms of lives and treasure are directly connected to the duration of the war and the insurgent resistance it produced. Democratic leaders might have asked Secretary of Defense Donald Rumsfeld—with an insistence not actually demonstrated—"What if there are no weapons of mass destruction and no ability to employ them, and what if Sunni Arabs and other dissident factions and foreign jihadists resort to insurgent warfare in the cities? How long will we maintain troops in Iraq and what will it cost?" And what if the questioners had not permitted the dismissive secretary to get by with his customary elusions of "We don't fight wars on what ifs," or "We don't know what we don't know but if we knew what we don't know we might not know what we know" gibberish.

An honest and straightforward administration would have responded, "We haven't planned for that contingency because we are totally confident it will not happen. If it does, we will apologize to the American people and expect to suffer the consequences in the next national election." Ah, but that kind of accountability is too much to expect in this age of responsibility avoidance and spin.

And, finally, *what about estimated casualties?* Those of us raising this question in the summer and fall of 2002 were met with ridicule from the administration and its media supporters and polite disdain from the leaders of our party. "No one can say," was the response. War is war, and war is hell. Though this kind of obfuscation seemed to mollify those Democrats inclined to accept easy assurances, it happens not to be true. War planners routinely make casualty estimates, on the low side and on the high side, according to a variety of scenarios favorable and unfavorable. Good military strategists and planners take into account all options, including worst-case ones. One of those scenarios, locked in a Pentagon safe (if not already shredded), had to do with a long-term, low-intensity urban insurgency.

An amateur strategist, I estimated American casualties—killed and wounded combined—under these conditions at five thousand to ten thousand. A much more serious and seasoned commander, General Barry McCaffrey, forecast as many as fifty thousand American casualties in a prolonged, insurgency-riddled American occupation. I was on the low side. Four years in, we are about halfway toward the McCaffrey estimate, with no end in sight.

Critics will say that to raise questions in a time of war about allied assistance, duration of hostilities and length of deployment, costs in dollars, and estimated casualties is to nitpick, to raise doubt, to undermine national security, to question the judgment of leaders, to erode national resolve, to display weakness and a lack of patriotism. But had the Democrats demonstrated courage, placed conviction over compromise, and been willing to challenge conventional wisdom and established authority—in the best American tradition, I might add—*the fallacies in the pro-war argument could have been revealed.*

There was little genuine evidence of weapons of mass destruction in Iraq. Rhetoric aside, there was no evidence of collaboration between Iraq and al Qaeda. There was a real possibility of insidious insurgency. There was an obvious opportunity for foreign jihadists, particularly from Saudi Arabia, to use the American occupation of an Islamic country as a rallying point for recruitment and as a training ground for future jihadists. A few lonely voices repeatedly predicted in 2002 and 2003 that by invading Iraq we were going to "kick open a hornets' nest," and it took no particular genius to say so. Now we are told we cannot leave until we have put all the hornets back into the nest. Think again.

If the opposition party, the Democrats, refused to oppose, what conceivably were their reasons? Several possibilities exist. The first and most obvious reason is that the Democrats were misled along with everyone else, including virtually all the Republicans. Here two more possibilities exist. Either the president was misled by the U.S. intelligence services, in which case those responsible should have been fired (but were not); or the president willingly and knowingly participated in a neoconservative "cabal" (as it was later called by Colonel Lawrence Wilkerson, Secretary of State Colin Powell's chief of staff) that systematically misled the American people. If so, the political consequences of this are stunning in their implications of dishonesty, lack of principle, and arrogance toward the sovereignty of the American people.

It took until late December 2005 for President Bush to finally accept responsibility, though not accountability, for the massively wrong intelligence concerning the presence of weapons of mass destruction and the threat posed by Iraq to America, and for the unanticipated consequences of a virulent domestic insurgency. The Democrats who followed George W. Bush down this path, for whatever reasons, without exercising greater skepticism can take little comfort from this reluctant and long-overdue shift by the president. They had a duty of care to ask tough questions and to deny support until those questions were answered. That duty is not one of partisanship. That duty is one of citizenship, leadership, and statesmanship.

Sufficient time has passed since the errors and dishonesty have surfaced for redemption to have occurred. In the face of such evidence of manipulation of intelligence, few Democrats stepped forward to say, at the least, "I was misled," or, at the most, "I was wrong." What has confounded rank-and-file Democrats and many independent voters is the stubborn refusal of many pro-invasion Democrats to say anything at all, whether mea culpa or apology.

Indeed, the only real "opposition" policy offered by Democratic leaders like Senators Hillary Clinton and Joseph Lieberman has been, "Up the ante. Commit more troops. Increase the U.S. military presence and the size of the occupation forces." This at a time when two-thirds of the American people and close to 90 percent of the Democratic Party's supporters have turned against the war and when it is increasingly clear to many that it is the very presence of American troops that provides strong stimulus to the insurgency.

Consider the times in which this catastrophe occurred. The twenty-first century's first sunrise revealed a nation adrift. The Cold War had come abruptly and unexpectedly to an end a decade earlier. Our central organizing principle—the containment of communism—had been rendered irrelevant, and for ten years we had very little comprehensive sense of where we as a nation were going. Democrats seemed no clearer than Republicans as to our purposes, objectives, and mission in the world. Sole superpower status offered virtually endless possibilities, perhaps too many. In 1990, Francis Fukuyama famously declared democracy's triumph as "the end of history," and by 2000 it seemed to many Americans that he was right.

But history has its own way of remaining obscure, opaque, and mysterious. And, missing the Cold War's peculiar clarity and knowing that it is easier to unite Americans *against* something than it is to unite us *for* something, the neoconservatives in the new Bush administration swiftly saw the "war on terrorism" as the Next Big Confrontation. It would require the passage of only a few months after the September 11 attacks before George W. Bush would be advocating a Middle East "crusade" against the rising threat of a new Caliphate, the term for an Islamic empire reaching from Gibraltar to Eastern Indonesia.

Within a year this new form of strategic clarity, the kind of clarity offered only by catastrophe, arose from the ashes of the World Trade Center, the twin-tower symbols of American commercial dominance finally brought down, on the second try, by the demented and determined al Qaeda, the spawn of the ferocious fundamentalists the United States had armed, trained, equipped, and financed to fight the Soviets in Afghanistan in the 1980s. The clarity of vengeance against the killers of three thousand American civilians united the nation and most of the world in our support to seek out our attackers and eliminate their hosts, the Taliban. The French newspaper *Le Monde* declared, "Today we are all Americans." No partisan issue arose for Democrats. Within days of 9/11, I wrote for the *Times* of London: "We will find Osama bin Laden. We will give him a fair trial. And then, as we did in the old West, we will hang him."

In the heat and passion of the moment it never occurred to many Americans that the long-standing obsession of senior figures in the Bush administration with Saddam Hussein might surface within a few months, perhaps even within a few weeks, to replace the imperative of capturing and hanging the killer of three thousand Americans. Though much evidence existed of this obsession, going back to the mid-1990s, it was simply inconceivable that the Bush administration would corner upwards of two thousand Taliban and al Qaeda, including Osama bin Laden, in Tora Bora in late 2001 and then let them escape while it began its monomaniacal preparation to overthrow Saddam Hussein and make Iraq the base for massive U.S. military dominance of the troubled Middle East.

Politically, 9/11 released the latent energies of neoconservatives, who had long dreamed of overthrowing Saddam

Hussein as an exercise in a new form of aggressive "democratic idealism," a rhetorical patina concealing the ambitions of empire. But the closed shop that was the Bush White House would reveal none of its more elaborate schemes, schemes requiring a Dostoyevsky to fathom. It would take years for the wheel to turn, for the imperial dream to be dashed against the realities of Iraq. In February 2006, Francis Fukuyama, often cited by the neoconservatives as an intellectual godfather of their movement, chided the neoconservatives in the Bush administration for having badly misunderstood the post–Cold War world, in an article clarifying his revised views in the *New York Times Magazine*. "The Bush doctrine [of preemptive invasions] that set the framework for the administration's first term," he observed, "is now in shambles."

Once again, however, the issue at hand is not the obsessions of the neoconservative Bush administration, but rather the response of the leaders of the Democratic Party to this abrupt, illogical, and ultimately groundless national security strategy. Some Democrats in office did not even bother to ask perfunctory questions but simply—to demonstrate "strength"—swallowed the radical, preemptive, unilateralist strategy hook, line, and sinker.

It is a very great mystery how the Democrats, known as the "war party" to isolationist conservative Republicans in mid-twentieth-century America, lost their interest and credibility in national security matters and lost them so hopelessly as to require them to endorse an unnecessary, unprincipled, and unprecedented invasion almost without question for fear of being seen as "weak." As someone who has spent three decades considering the question and trying to answer it in constructive ways, it all seems to come back to Vietnam.

After the end of that war, very few Democrats seemed to want to touch matters having to do with the military, and if they did, it was either to oppose new weapons systems or to resist the use of force. Even when Democratic leaders undertook military operations, as in the failed hostage rescue mission in Iran in 1980, they were ill-fated. There have been exceptions, of course, but overall it seemed that things tended to go badly anytime Democrats got near the military. Early in his term President Bill Clinton was even ridiculed for not knowing the proper way to salute the marine officer at the foot of his helicopter steps.

September 11 changed things for the Democrats. The country had drifted for almost exactly a decade from the collapse of the Soviet Union in 1991 without serious challenge to our security, but now, instantly, all America seemed vulnerable to bloodthirsty terrorists. If members of the opposition party already had the reputation for being "weak on defense," how were they to respond when the administration declared Iraq to be the "central front" of the war on terrorism and the greatest threat to our national security since the Soviet Union? The easy political course was to go along. It just happened not to be the courageous, or patriotic, course.

Having gone along in large numbers with the Iraqi invasion, what then should be the response of those pro-war Democrats when, three years later, the casus belli, the justification for war, has evaporated into thin air, the occupation has turned stagnant and nasty, and the American people have abandonded their support for the war in large numbers? One would think that these Democrats would at long last begin to ask serious questions, make statements against the occupation—if nothing else, in support of our troops who are being killed and professionally decimated with little justification—and offer a way out. But, with a few important exceptions, they did not.

In fact, too many senior Democrats have continued to support the harsh (and probably unconstitutional) measures such as torture of prisoners and mass eavesdropping on Americans that the war of occupation has spawned. A half dozen Democrats provided the margin of victory for a 2005 Republican-sponsored law denying prisoners at Guantánamo Bay, Cuba, the right to challenge the legality of their endless incarceration in federal court. "A foreign national who is captured and determined to be an enemy combatant in the world war on terrorism," said Senator Joseph Lieberman in justification of his vote, has no right of appeal under the U.S. Constitution.

But of course Senator Lieberman missed the point: Who has the authority to determine who is and is not an "enemy combatant"? This law "consigns the protection of fundamental human liberties to unilateral executive determination," a group of influential legal scholars said in a letter urging the Senate to reject the bill. Senator Lieberman and many other Democrats were willing to let George W. Bush be judge and jury long after most Americans began to doubt the wisdom, let alone the legality, of such a policy.

Senator Lieberman and other Democrats clearly had not learned the lessons of the French occupations of Indochina and Algeria, the last of France's fading empire, and the brutal measures even a civilized occupier resorts to in order to combat indigenous insurgents using terrorist methods to force foreign occupiers out of their countries.

Inevitably, the excuses of wartime would be used to justify unconstitutional behavior. In December 2005, news reports forced President Bush to admit that he had authorized the National Security Agency (and undoubtedly the whole panoply of intelligence collection agencies) to intercept the communications of American citizens on a massive scale, without recourse to judicial authorization by special security courts as required by U.S. law under the Fourth Amendment to the Constitution, which states, "The right of the people to be secure in their persons, houses, papers, and effects, against unreasonable searches and seizures, shall not be violated, and *no Warrants shall issue, but upon probable cause, supported by Oath or affirmation*, and particularly describing the place to be searched, and the persons or things to be seized." (Emphasis added.) In justifying this violation of constitutional rights the president seemed able to convince himself that he was operating within the law even when it was clear he was not.

This is extraordinary. Almost as extraordinary was the fact that the political party that had carried the burden of defending America throughout most of the twentieth century had gone mute or was willing to follow a badly misled or misleading president back into the Big Muddy. "Waist deep in the Big Muddy and the big fool said to push on," warned an anti–Vietnam war song many years ago. How could this be?

Like the cat that jumped on a hot stove and thereafter wouldn't jump on any stove hot or cold, today's Democratic Party leaders do not want to make the mistake that they feel has brought about the party's electoral decline—its embrace of the antiwar movement, embodied in the 1972 presidential campaign of George McGovern, which I know something about. Many supported the Iraq war resolution and, as the Big Muddy has risen yet again, find themselves tongue-tied or trying to trump a war president by calling for deployment of more troops.

History will deal with George W. Bush and the neoconservatives who misled a mighty nation into a flawed war that is draining the finest military in the world, diverting National Guard and Army Reserve forces that should be the front line of homeland defense, shredding international alliances that prevailed in two world wars and the Cold War, accumulating staggering deficits, misdirecting revenues from education to rebuilding Iraqi buildings we've blown up, and weakening America's national security.

But what will history say about an opposition party that stood silent while all this went on? My generation of Democrats jumped on the hot stove of Vietnam and now, its members in positions of responsibility, is afraid of jumping on any political stove hot or cold, including one badly requiring serious attention. In their leaders, the American people look for strength, determination, and self-confidence, but they also look for courage, wisdom, judgment, and, in times of moral crisis, the willingness to say, "I was wrong."

To stay silent during such a crisis, and particularly to harbor the thought that the administration's misfortune is the Democrats' fortune, is cowardly. In 2008, the American people will look for a leader who was willing to say, "I made a mistake. And for my mistake I am going to Iraq and accompany the next planeload of flag-draped coffins back to Dover Air Force Base, and I am going to ask forgiveness for my mistake from every parent who will talk to me."

And further, this leader would say, "I am now going to give a series of speeches across the country documenting how the administration did not tell the American people the truth, why this war is making our country more vulnerable and less secure, how we can drive a wedge between Iraqi insurgents and outside jihadists and leave Iraq for the Iraqis to govern, how we can repair the damage done to our military, what we and our allies can do to dry up the jihadists' swamp, and dramatic steps we need to take to become energy secure and prevent Gulf Wars III, IV," and so on.

At stake is not just the leadership of the Democratic Party or even the nation. At stake are our nation's honor, our nobility, and our principles. Franklin Roosevelt established a national community based on social justice. Harry Truman created international networks that repaired the damage of World War II and defeated communism. John Kennedy recaptured the ideal of the republic and the sense of civic duty. Lyndon Johnson recognized that all citizens are entitled to equality before the law. To expect to enter this pantheon, the next Democratic leader must now undertake all these tasks.

But this cannot be done while the water is rising in the Big Muddy of the Middle East, our twenty-first-century Vietnam-in-the-desert. No Democrat, especially one who remains silent when conviction requires a voice, should expect election by default. The public trust must be earned, and speaking clearly, candidly, and forcefully about the quagmire in Iraq is the place to begin. Instead, too many Democrats are huddled in silence, awaiting the call of Paul Revere well after the redcoats have occupied their colony.

The real defeatists today are not those protesting the war. The defeatists are those in power and their silent supporters in the opposition party who are reduced to chanting "stay the course" even when the "course," whatever it now is, is light-years away from the course that was undertaken. The truth is, we've lost the course. We've kicked open a hornets' nest with consequences yet to be felt in America. We've weakened ourselves at home and in the world. We are less secure today than before this war began.

Who now has the courage to say this?

A number of Democratic leaders finally came to do so in the fall of 2005. Senator John Kerry, the Democratic nominee in 2004, whose perceived ambivalence on Iraq (though shared by the nation) was made to seem indecisive by his opponents, was an initial voice speaking forcefully at Georgetown University in October 2005. He spoke of the mistaken war and what an alternative strategy might contain. His vice presidential running mate, former senator John Edwards, soon followed with his own admission of mistaken trust in the administration. Then others, including former president Bill Clinton, called the war "wrong." A slow and somewhat sad parade of party leaders recanted their trust in a misled or misleading president.

But, of course, by the end of 2005 any Democrat still supporting the war would easily have been entranced by Scheherazade.

I have treated Iraq at length not because it is the cause of confusion in the Democratic Party but rather because it is a symptom of that confusion. Had my party found its compass and set its course at the end of the Cold War, using the fixed principles so important to twentieth-century

America, Iraq would have been treated much differently by early-twenty-first-century Democrats. Arguments for preventive or preemptive invasion would have been met with much more scrutiny and healthy skepticism because Democrats would have had their own defense policy based on military reform, "fourth generation" warfare, human intelligence, cooperative threat reduction, and resistance to foreign adventurism.

To justify a restoration of public trust, much more will be required of the dormant Democratic Party than the simple recantation of support for an unnecessary war. The party must reconnect with its days of dominance, direction, and some glory if it is to find its way to the beginning of wisdom. There are reasons why throughout most of the twentieth century the Democratic Party was a great party, a party that had the support and confidence of a majority of the American people. That history offers invaluable mileposts in the restoration of public support for Democratic Party leadership in the new century that is still but a few years old.

2

THE PARTY OF TIMIDITY

What brought the great Democratic Party, the majority party for much of the twentieth century—the party of Woodrow Wilson and Franklin Delano Roosevelt, the party of Harry Truman, John F. Kennedy, and Lyndon Johnson, the party that successfully led the nation through two world wars and much of the Cold War, the party of the New Deal and the Great Society, the party of great figures and instinctive visionaries, the political home of most of the grand thinking of the twentieth century, the party of civil rights and gender equality, the party that rescued America from the Great Depression, the party of the blue-collar working class and desperate Dust Bowl farmers, the party that provided the ladder of opportunity for generations of immigrants, the party of virtually all progressive movements for a century—what caused that great and historic political institution to cave in so quickly and so willingly to the most questionable military adventure since the invasion of the Philippines a century before?

Equally, what brought some representatives of the party of working people, left-out people, unemployed people, small farmers and business people to support economic policies clearly designed to enrich the rich and to shift wealth further upward? Was the party so bereft of ideas as to how to use globalization and information to make the economic pie expand and distribute its wealth more widely and fairly that it had no choice but to support lightening the tax burden of the most privileged among us? And were Democrats who voted to effectively eliminate regulations on toxic waste disposal, worker safety, and pension protection so callous toward the victims of these excesses and so lacking in respect for the hard-won social gains paid for by previous generations of Democrats, so nervous for their careers, that they rolled over to the phony "free market" arguments of corrupting corporate lobbyists?

This is not a book about the Iraq war, nor is it meant principally as a critique of the Bush administration's catastrophic misadventures in the Middle East, nor is it even an attempt to identify the date when Democrats abandoned the ideal that effective government could make our nation better. It is an attempt to discover the roots of drift, weakness, and capitulation in the Democratic Party of the early twenty-first century.

The meek surrender of half the Democrats in the Senate and the House when the war trumpets sounded is but a metaphor for a larger question: Is the Democratic Party only temporarily unmoored and adrift, or has it become rudderless and dismasted? Are there, to shift the metaphor, some serious, systemic, long-term diseases afflicting, possibly eroding, the very roots of the oldest political party in the world?

This is not a new concern. In an epilogue to my first book, *Right from the Start: A Chronicle of the McGovern Campaign*, written a third of a century ago, I concluded, "The fount of specific proposals and programs was running dry. The party's traditional sources of invigorating, inspiring, and creative ideas were dissipating. The best thinkers of the 1930s, 40s, and 50s and even the 1960s were not producing. . . . By 1972, American liberalism was near bankruptcy."

A presidential campaign based principally on opposition to the American war in Vietnam was not also prepared to address an economy that had become stagnant, the competition between guns and butter the war had produced, questions regarding more efficient administration of social programs, the rusting of our industrial base, the challenge of foreign competition, the environmental legacy of industrial waste, the expanding demands by minorities and women for more political and economic participation, the questions of where and when American military power should be employed, and what seemed like an endless host of problems that had been deferred or never before confronted.

The liberal party, the progressive party, the party of ideas, innovation, and creativity, had run out of gas.

This historic fact was thereafter obscured by episodes and interventions that deferred the day of political reckoning for Democrats. The disaster of Watergate and the Nixon impeachment gave the Democratic Party breathing room during which a new generation of candidates, including myself, was elected, and Jimmy Carter won the presidency on the promise of restoring integrity to the White House. The end of the Cold War in 1991 permitted Bill Clinton, a governor without defense or foreign-policy credentials, to occupy the White House for eight years. But even then he lacked strong election mandates and for six years was shackled by Republican majorities in Congress preventing innovation in any far-reaching way in serious domestic crises such as health care.

With these notable exceptions, the past forty years have not been good ones for the Democratic Party, especially when compared with the age of Democratic dominance that lasted from 1932 to 1968—the Roosevelt, Truman, Kennedy, and Johnson years. (Dwight Eisenhower's two terms were moderate years and did not disrupt the larger political trend.) These were the years of the Great Depression and World War II, the Marshall Plan and the reconstruction of Europe and Asia, the dawn of the Cold War, the containment of communism and the Korean war, the "ask not" generation and the Cuban missile crisis.

And then, abruptly, things began to unravel and run amok. Presidents, presidential candidates, and civil rights leaders were assassinated. A half million American military forces went upriver in Vietnam, into the heart of darkness, and more than fifty thousand never came back alive. Foreign-made cars arrived on our shores and the great steel mills, auto assembly lines, and industrial boilers from Gary, Indiana, to Buffalo, New York, first shut down and grew cold, then rusted almost overnight. First the Democratic Party and then the nation divided and fractured over Vietnam, in some cases irreparably.

Hawkish Democrats, traditionally disdainful of Republican isolationism and supportive of the Democratic war presidents—Roosevelt, Truman, Kennedy, and Johnson—in the wake of the Vietnam morass found the party in the hands of loathsome "McGovernites" and found Richard Nixon more to their liking. Within a decade these Democrats found it convenient to become Reagan Republicans. The solid Democratic South, during this same period of the mid- and late 1960s, also suddenly confronted two new realities, a Democratic Party leadership increasingly opposed to the Vietnam war and, perhaps more important, a Democratic Party no longer willing to tolerate racial segregation as the price for maintaining electoral majorities.

As if all this turmoil were not enough for any single

period of history, half the population, American women, decided now was the time to assert their claim to equal economic and political rights. Better educated now, and liberated by birth control pills, new household appliances, and increasing job opportunities, women insisted on equal footing in political participation—especially in the more progressive Democratic Party—and in the employment marketplace. Besides, with the economy now beginning to stagnate, middle-class families found that they required two wage earners just to maintain their standard of living.

By championing civil rights the Democratic Party forfeited its political base in the South and alienated white males, especially in labor unions, who saw their jobs threatened by minorities entering the job market. By championing the rights of women, the Democratic Party further alienated men who now had to compete not only with minority males but also with women of all colors.

Additionally, the late 1960s and early 1970s were years in which federal government regulation increased appreciably, usually with just cause. When Rachel Carson lifted the lid on the cesspool of environmental degradation with her book *Silent Spring* in 1962, the chickens from decades of unrestricted industrial air and water pollution came home to roost. A decade later, the Love Canal case and the poisoning of real people in real neighborhoods made the heritage of pollution from the industrial age human, graphic, and immediate.

Congress rushed to enact clean air, clean water, and

toxic waste disposal laws, created an Environmental Protection Agency, and empowered it to issue regulations under the laws to protect the American people. Labor unions and their members became fed up with unsafe working conditions and demanded laws and regulations to protect them from employers who perpetuated dangerous workplaces as a means of boosting the profit bottom line. The consumer movement arose demanding elimination of dangerous products, better food labeling, safer toys for children, and safer automobiles for the family. The great regulatory era had arrived and the environment, workplaces, and consumer products all became safer, cleaner, and more protected.

It would not be long, however, before each of these movements toward social progress crested, then generated a political backlash. Eager regulators swept small businesses into their nets along with Fortune 500 companies and demanded equal compliance. Small farmers would confront costly and cumbersome restrictions on their operations. Large manufacturers shut down when challenged by foreign competitors. The regulatory era, while making life for tens of millions safer and cleaner, took its economic, then its political toll. Few who benefited credited the Democratic Party for its leadership. Virtually all who were required to comply blamed the Democrats.

It would not take long before a variety of isolated backlashes from neoconservatives, white males, labor members, regulated industries, and prowar, promilitary interventionists would coalesce into one big backlash against a Democratic Party now seen as weak, antidefense, peacenik, regulation-ridden, welfare-giveaway-oriented, women-dominated, and minority-controlled.

Ironically, even as this great backlash was cresting, in 1976 the Republican candidate for vice president, Robert Dole, would argue during a televised debate that if you wanted to go to war, vote Democratic. Dole was still stuck in the Midwest Republican isolationist tradition, which castigated the Democrats (Wilson, Roosevelt, Truman, Kennedy, Johnson) for leading the country into foreign wars. Dole's warning was badly out of date and, in retrospect, almost comical. He was preaching disengagement when the backlash mood of the country was bellicose.

Two major revolutions further challenged Democratic tradition—globalization and information. Globalization, the internationalization of finance, commerce, and trade, brought a flood tide of foreign products to America's shores, products approximating American quality but at cheaper prices. Steel, automobiles, clothing and textiles, television sets and home appliances, wristwatches, and a cornucopia of foreign products suddenly swamped store shelves. American manufacturers closed down or moved offshore to find cheap labor. American labor unions began a long, uninterrupted decline in membership and, in desperation, turned to the Democratic Party to rescue them with protectionist legislation. In the meantime, the very foundation of the

United States economy was shifting away from manufacturing to information, communications, and high technology.

The response of the last generation of New Deal Democrats to these tidal shifts was to undertake a last-ditch stand in support of the great social advances of the 1930s, '40s, '50s, and '60s by refusing to streamline public assistance programs, make the burgeoning regulatory state more efficient, resist destructive protectionism, challenge their traditional constituent groups to adapt to these revolutions in any constructive way, or create policies to use the new information economy to expand the economic pie. The net effect was to make the party of progress, innovation, and imagination a party of reactionary liberalism. In an era of radical change, we Democrats began to look like the party of the past, the party of the status quo, the conservative party. In our resistance to redefinition, we acquired all the worst traits of the Republican Party.

Worse yet, because of the deep trauma and schism of the Vietnam war, we Democrats were no longer the party of national security.

But the end of the Cold War did permit a young, attractive, and charismatic Democratic governor, Bill Clinton, to "feel your pain" and finally fulfill George McGovern's admonition to "come home, America." He offered the hope of attention to a long-deferred domestic agenda, particularly health care delivery and cost, and healing of lingering racial divides. But the complex health care industry, composed of insurers, service providers, hospitals, doctors, nurses, and many others, had its own ideas about how to fix the problem, and all those ideas were contradictory and self-defeating.

To break out of the stagnant and unproductive left-right stalemate, Clinton adopted "centrism" through "triangulation." By the time anyone really began to figure out what that meant, the Clinton years had fled by, leaving behind a coterie of Clintonistas sitting cross-legged on the floor of the party headquarters trying to put the pieces back together like amateur magicians contemplating the bust of Houdini.

Some mystery rhetoric about the "vital center" may have been sufficient to see Bill Clinton through the interim between the Cold War and the war on terrorism, but it did not leave in its wake a set of principles upon which to base a political party in a new century. Tactics can never compensate for lack of strategy. Indeed, by the time the dust settled, the smoke dissipated, and the mirrors were crated, centrism seemed merely a way station where the principles underlying the governments of Roosevelt, Truman, Kennedy, and Johnson might be stored without having to bring them out, dust them off, and make them applicable to a new century and a new age.

By seeking to avoid the stalemate of rigid ideology through a strategy of triangulation and centrism, the Clinton Democrats also forfeited principle and conviction—and the nobility that comes from both. Triangulation and centrism are tactical positioning maneuvers but are not a basis for governing. To construct a governing philosophy, a platform for statecraft, is hard work, work that has been left undone for a generation.

At the very least, statecraft requires a sense of history, a sense of purpose and mission, a set of principles and the ability to operate pragmatically within them, deep dedication to achieving a degree of national progress, belief in effective government, and the ability to see over the horizon. Specific government programs are not required but are rather the product of that governing philosophy, that principled manifesto. Franklin Roosevelt was the ultimate pragmatist. He did not enter the White House with the blueprint of the New Deal under his arm. He was willing to try almost any experiment to get the nation back on its feet, discarding those that did not work and keeping those that did.

Statecraft also requires the ability to adapt to new realities. The post–Cold War world turned out to be more problematic than anyone might have imagined. The collapse of the Soviet Union simply took the bipolar, democratic-versus-communist lid off a messy world. Nations began to fail. Religious fundamentalism, ethnic nationalism, and antique tribalism filled the vacuum of ideology. Weapons of mass destruction entered their own global market virtually overnight. Mass migration from the poor south in Latin America and North Africa to a prosperous north in North America and Europe greedy for cheap labor became tidal in scope. Tribes, clans, and gangs filled the vacuum created by failed and failing states and began to assert authority and co-opt the nation-state monopoly on violence.

Most of all, radical Islamic terrorism, largely originating during the war against the Soviet Union in Afghanistan in the 1980s, came to visit the United States with the first World Trade Center bombing in 1993. The irony of America's massive support for the Afghan mujahedeen, some of whose tribal and religious factions became the Taliban in the 1990s, has been widely noted by such authors as George Crile (in *Charlie Wilson's War*) and Steve Coll (in *Ghost Wars*).

In the context of this uncertain new world and at the dawn of an equally uncertain new century, in 2000 America experienced one of the closest national elections in its history, with the electoral college outcome uncertain for five weeks. The nation could not decide whether it was liberal or conservative, in part because both political parties and their candidates were desperately contesting for the "center," a locus much favored by media pundits and political consultants but which not one of them can clearly define.

In the quarter century following the end of the Vietnam war in 1975, few Democrats could be found who would take the time and trouble to study military history, to understand military reform principles and ideas, to comprehend force structures, to know why some weapons systems made no sense and others, often less costly, were more effective in combat, to learn why the French, who had more men under arms and more tanks than the Germans, nevertheless fell in forty days in 1940, to learn the real lessons of Vietnam, to understand the absolute necessity of unit cohesion in combat, to learn the difference between maneuver and attrition warfare, to be able to refute the folly of a national missile shield, to accept the closing of redundant military bases, to find the courage to resist the industrial and labor lobbyists who insisted on using gigantic weapons projects as public-works jobs programs.

The Democratic Party that led us through two world wars, Korea, the Cuban missile crisis, and much of the Cold War mysteriously succumbed to amnesia on national security matters. And if not amnesia, then some kind of rash where military matters were concerned. To his credit, President Clinton finally did intervene in the Balkans in 1999 through bombing to save the Kosovars from genocide. But we had previously withdrawn from our humanitarian mission in Somalia, under widespread public pressure, when sixteen Americans were killed in Mogadishu. And we had refused, tragically, to intervene to prevent the slaughter of eight hundred thousand Tutsis in Rwanda. And even in the Balkans, we had stood by as atrocities were committed in Bosnia from 1992 to 1995.

George W. Bush drifted into the White House, barely, as the century turned, with no particular sense of America's role in the world. Then came 9/11, the war on terrorism, and the detour into the Iraqi swamp that so silenced much of the Democratic Party's leadership.

"Centrism" as a governing philosophy was a light that failed. It lacked principle. It lacked conviction. It did not offer a platform on which to demonstrate any kind of political courage. It was a political tactic, not a platform for statecraft or a governing philosophy that established firm guidelines for determining when force should, and should not, be used.

Without the credentials in military and national security affairs required to establish authority and credibility, and against the backdrop of a quarter century of drift on security-related matters, too many Democrats lacked the rudder, compass, and set of charts required to steer into Afghanistan and on to Tora Bora and to avoid the shoals, sandbars, and reefs of Fallujah, Najaf, and Sadr City in Baghdad.

Party leaders emerge by achieving leadership positions in the houses of Congress or by conducting presidential campaigns sufficiently successful to capture the party's presidential nomination or to demonstrate widespread public appeal during the nomination process. Though the votes of Democratic Party members in the House and Senate on the Iraq war resolution in October 2002 were decidedly divided between those who favored and those who opposed, in the case of House Democrats it was 81 yeas and 126 nays and among Senate Democrats there were 29 yeas and 21 nays. Significant were the leading Senate Democrats who supported the resolution: Hillary Clinton, the former first lady;

John Kerry, the future 2004 Democratic presidential nominee; John Edwards, the future 2004 vice presidential nominee; Evan Bayh, a presumed presidential candidate in 2008; Joseph Biden, a former chairman of the Foreign Relations Committee and another potential 2008 candidate; Tom Daschle, the Senate Democratic majority leader; Ernest Hollings, a candidate for the presidential nomination in 1984; Joseph Lieberman, the Democratic vice presidential candidate in 2000 and a 2004 contender; Harry Reid, the future Senate Democratic minority leader; and twenty others. Those voting in the negative included a number of visible Democrats such as Edward Kennedy, Robert C. Byrd, Patrick Leahy, Carl Levin, Bob Graham, Russell Feingold, and fifteen others.

Hindsight is, of course, the clearest form of sight. At issue here is not a roll call of who was right and who was wrong, though several of those Democrats who voted in the affirmative have belatedly disclaimed their votes, and given the absence of Iraq's weapons of mass destruction, connection to al Qaeda, or threat to the United States, the negative votes look prescient. At issue now is the legitimacy or lack thereof of those who supported the war and now remain silent. The question is one of courage, conviction, and genuine leadership. In such situations it is always helpful to remind ourselves of Dante's well-known assertion: "There is a special place in Hell for those who, in times of moral crisis, preserve their neutrality."

There may also be a special place in political hell for those Democratic leaders who covet the presidency but refuse to promote, with any degree of intensity, a thoughtful, effective, and realistic exit plan from Iraq. The price of silence now will be the forfeiture of the party's nomination in 2008.

Finding itself adrift and tempted to accommodate to errant policies in its desire for acceptance, the Democratic Party might well consider revisiting the best of its past and searching less for power and more for principle. When a political party acquires the confidence of a majority of the American people, there are usually good reasons for it, and those reasons almost always have to do with what it stands for, what it believes in, what it treasures. Those principles are not transient. They abide. Properly adapted, they are as good in one age as they have proved to be in another.

3

KNOWING WHERE WE CAME FROM

When one is adrift and seeking direction, the best course is often to return to the point of origin, the port of embarkation, to recover both the charts and the compass created, in this case, by the Democratic Party's great captains—Franklin Roosevelt, Harry Truman, John Kennedy, and Lyndon Johnson. Pragmatists will ask, "What made them successful? How did they win?" Idealists will ask, "What did they know about their party—and, more important, their country—that enabled them to lead, each in his own way, through perilous times?"

All should ask, "What principles were there in their respective governing philosophies that might reestablish a foundation under the Democratic Party of the twenty-first century?"

Franklin Roosevelt and the Idea of Community and Social Justice

Franklin Roosevelt, as noted, was anything but an ideologue. He was one of the great pragmatic leaders in American history. Few would argue that he entered office in 1933 with a programmatic blueprint for saving America from the worst economic depression in our history. Nor could it be argued that Roosevelt was an intellectual genius. Indeed, the respected Cold War historian John Lewis Gaddis argues in his book *Surprise, Security, and the American Experience* that Roosevelt lowered the intellectual bar for the presidency to a point where even George W. Bush could qualify as a great strategist.

What Roosevelt did possess in considerable quantity was a sense of the American character, a genius for direct communication, and a view to the nation's historical role in the world. He also operated on certain immutable principles. We are one nation, one society, one community. When large numbers of us are ill-clothed, ill-fed, and ill-housed, all of us suffer. We believe in justice. It is wrong for the powerful and the wealthy to profit unjustly at the expense of the rest of us. We are part of a larger world community. If fascism, tyranny, and imperialism threaten other democratic nations, we cannot stand idly by.

What Roosevelt left behind, now neglected in an age of conservatism, individualism, and personal autonomy, were the ideals of social cohesion, national community, and international engagement. Democrats came to worship in the cathedral of the New Deal, seeking to preserve specific social programs, bureaucratic structures, and outdated methodologies, well into the 1960s and '70s when, had he been alive, Roosevelt himself would have said, "Keep the ideals and the principles, but find new ways to achieve them."

The "centrism" of the 1990s involved Democrats' unnecessarily throwing the baby out with the bathwater. Middle-income Americans did turn against "waste, fraud, and abuse," an antigovernment slogan that conveniently went into hiding during Republican administrations, but they did not turn against the poor. And, contrary to the Clinton formulation, they did not turn against government as such. Instead, they turned against *ineffective* government. To its credit, the Clinton administration did establish programs to make the national government more effective, such as the National Performance Review, created to identify and eliminate waste, fraud, and abuse in federal programs and to reduce redundant regulation and bureaucracy.

Starting in the late 1960s and early 1970s, however, if Democrats had adopted national policies to ease the shift from manufacturing to information and help workers and communities make that transition, if we had found ways to use new technologies to make a stagnant economic pie expand instead of using protectionist measures to stand in the doorway of progress, if we had insisted on more efficient administration of public assistance programs, if we had declared a new era of *effective* government instead of abandoning Roosevelt's commitment to social justice by declaring the era of "big government" to be over, then the Democratic Party could have maintained its middle-class base, continued to be the voice of conscience in America, and preserved the principled foundation laid down by Franklin Roosevelt.

Instead, we continued to worship in the New Deal cathedral even as we abandoned the social gospel upon which it was founded. Our political faith became ritualistic, programmatic, bureaucratic, and rigidly ideological in much the same way that some religious movements maintain the dogma, the rituals, and the liturgies long after they forget the purposes for which they were created. Even if we declare the era of big government to be over—and Roosevelt never set out to create a big government—we do not have to forfeit our dedication to *effective* government.

Harry Truman and the Ideal of International Alliance

Harry Truman was caricatured in his day as a bumbler, an incompetent and small-bore rustic, especially when measured against the giant he so abruptly was required to replace. But Truman knew who he was and what he believed.

Though he relied on those Roosevelt advisers who stuck with him, and elevated some like Dean Acheson and George Marshall to large tasks, there is no record that Truman hired political consultants, conducted public opinion polls, or even could conceive of the need for "focus groups" to tell him what to think, say, or believe. He had a core set of principles that he brought with him to the presidency because they had guided him throughout his life. He was a self-confident man because he was a strong man.

Truman, first of all, could not abide the violation of the public trust. He came to public notice as a U.S. senator during World War II, holding a series of hearings that exposed waste and corruption in wartime procurement contracting. His sensitivity on these issues was no doubt heightened by the perception that he was the product of the corrupt Pendergast political machine in Kansas City. But Truman was proud to point out to an interlocutor, Merle Miller, late in life that when he left the White House he did not even take a pencil. "It didn't belong to me," he explained; "it belonged to the people of the United States."

More important for history, his military service in World War I as an artillery officer, his service as senator and vice president during World War II, and the unavoidable global agenda that fell in his lap in April 1945 all made the rustic clothing salesman an internationalist. But Truman's internationalism was a far cry from the aggressive, neoconservative, crypto-imperialist internationalism fashionable today.

It would take the form of a doctrine declaring Greece and Turkey off limits to communist takeover. It would create an Atlantic alliance, the North Atlantic Treaty Organization, declaring Western Europe off limits to Soviet expansion. It would embrace a Marshall Plan to reconstruct Germany and rebuild Western Europe and a similar effort to restructure Japan and stabilize a war-torn Asia. But the idea of imposing democracy on a vast and complex Arab culture at the point of a bayonet would never have occurred to him.

Significantly, Truman's internationalism was alliance-based and collaborative, not unilateralist; supportive, not interventionist; and based on containment, not preemption. It relied as much on the United States' economic and political strengths as it did on our military dominance.

Roosevelt almost single-handedly brought the United States into World War II, against strong Republican isolationist sentiments, and he is curiously still reviled for it in some reactionary circles. Truman was well aware of these political realities when the war ended. Faced with a choice of retreating from Europe and Asia and withdrawing to our protective island shield in North America, or maintaining our engagement in both theaters and accepting confrontation with communism in both venues, Truman, again in the face of considerable opposition, chose the latter. More than any other American, Harry Truman decided that we had no choice but to remain the world's leader for democracy.

As Roosevelt established a Democratic heritage of social justice and national community, Truman established a Democratic heritage of international engagement, coalition, and alliance.

John Kennedy and the Ideal of the Republic

John Kennedy's brief presidency, representing a generational shift from leadership by World War II generals to leadership by World War II lieutenants, is noted primarily for two things: the Cuban missile crisis and the iconic exhortation, "Ask not what your country can do for you; ask what you can do for your country." And, of course, it is remembered for its tragic ending.

Historically, the management of the missile crisis offered lessons for generations yet to come. By resisting the bluster of senior military officers, specifically Air Force General Curtis LeMay, to initiate massive military action against Cuba, and then against the Soviet Union if it came to Cuba's defense, and by resisting the softer suggestions of other advisers to avoid, at all costs, confrontation with the Soviet Union, Kennedy offered a textbook solution that combined diplomacy and force and a skillful understanding of history, the Soviet mentality, and the nature of the limits of a superpower's influence worthy of much older, more experienced, but perhaps not wiser world leaders.

Hopefully, the day will not come when a combination of

all those qualities will be required of a president faced with an ultimatum issued by some future al Qaeda that claims to have a pistol aimed at the head of Uncle Sam, a pistol that will be withdrawn only after an unacceptable acquiescence by the United States.

Beyond this powerful lesson in the use of both force and diplomacy, however, the Kennedy legacy to the party rests in the oft-repeated, but rarely appreciated, challenge to give something back to our country that has given us so much. Like Roosevelt's social compact and Truman's international engagement, Kennedy's challenge could only have been provided by a Democrat. The Republican Party of Franklin Roosevelt's age and of today does not believe in a government committed to social justice. The Republican Party of Harry Truman's age and of today does not believe in international alliances and institutions. The Republican Party of John Kennedy's time and of today certainly does not believe in national service or any organized participation by citizens in government.

Consciously or unconsciously, Kennedy's "ask not" challenge has echoed throughout the history of republics for twenty-five hundred years. From the days of ancient Athens through America's founding era, the hallmark of the republic has always been civic virtue, what today we would call civic duty and citizen participation. Ancient Greek and Roman republicans, and their successors in Machiavelli's Renaissance republican restoration, in the Venetian city-state, and in the Swiss cantons, down to the democratic republicans who formed the new federated republic of the United States, all have known that a republic cannot long survive if its citizens refuse to participate in self-governance, reject their citizen duties, or fundamentally want government, *their* government, to leave them alone.

What Kennedy restored, and twentieth-century Democrats instinctively knew, was the basic principle that our government either belongs to us, the people, or it belongs to powerful political and financial interests that take what they want from the public larder and then reject any role for that government in addressing the larger interests and concerns of the greater society.

In its purest forms the republican ideal is incompatible with the libertarian and laissez-faire impulse whose home has been in the Republican Party following the age of Theodore Roosevelt and the Progressives. (Indeed, Theodore Roosevelt's alienation from the Republican Party in 1912 was the result of those elements' rejection of his activist government policies.) If you want the national government to secure the nation's borders and provide protection for your property, and otherwise to leave you alone, you will probably not feel compelled to stir yourself from your comfortable gated fortress even once a month to attend to the public's business in the *ecclesia* or *campus martius* with your fellow citizens (the Greek and Roman forums, respectively, for conducting the republic's business). And this will be particularly true if you think some public project requiring public financing through the imposition of any kind of tax on wealth may be discussed.

By calling on Americans to ask what they could do for their country, Kennedy aroused in Americans the dormant spirit of the ancient Greek city-state. Almost a half century later it is important to note, unlike our more contemporary Democratic "centrists," that he did not feel compelled to declare the end of big government. Indeed, he offered public service through the Peace Corps and other avenues as a means of fulfilling one's republican duties and demonstrating civic virtue.

Ironically, almost exactly twenty years after Kennedy's "ask not" inaugural challenge, a Republican president would declare that "government is the problem." It would be too much to ask, one supposes, for Ronald Reagan to have understood why our founders insisted on using the language and ideals of the classic republic in their debates and institutional constructs or even why we salute the flag of the United States "and the republic for which it stands." It is a contradiction, to say the very least, to marginalize and demean the very government over which one successfully sought to preside, and then to challenge one's fellow citizens to fulfill their citizen duties by participating in its affairs, according to the classic principles of the republic, at the same time.

No, to be a republican requires some belief in participation, citizen governance, and civic virtue. Indeed, it requires a belief in the very process and institution of government. It requires a belief that government remains the primary institution for the collective conduct of the public's business. It requires an even more fundamental belief that government is of the people, by the people, and for the people. Since the age of Theodore Roosevelt, these have not been the beliefs of the Republican Party.

Only a party that believes in government—effective, efficient, and participatory government—can claim the true republican mantle. By pandering to antigovernment sentiments through the declaration of the end of "big government," whatever that was supposed in practice to mean, "centrist" Democratic Party leaders have sacrificed a portion of their rightful claim to the republican ideal at the core of America's founding. Besides, it is impossible to recall Franklin Roosevelt, Harry Truman, John Kennedy, or Lyndon Johnson specifically advocating "big government," so it is more than unclear exactly whose claim on behalf of big government is being rejected.

Lyndon Johnson and the Imperative of Equal Rights

Though he was a conservative southwestern Democrat, Lyndon Johnson's attitudes toward the role of government in our society were overwhelmingly shaped by Depression-era hardships and the responses of the New Deal. In his early years in Congress, Johnson was one of Franklin Roosevelt's strongest supporters. And he capitalized on New Deal programs of rural electrification, agricultural conservation, public works projects, and a host of other bootstrap policies to benefit his own district, eventually the state of Texas, and then, in the 1960s, the entire nation. In his time as Senate majority leader in the 1950s, Johnson discovered and in many cases created military and space contracts as the new military-industrial replacement for Roosevelt's public works projects. And by the time Johnson became president in 1963, Texas had become a national bastion of defense production and space exploration.

Johnson, this curious amalgam of New Deal liberal and southwestern conservative, faced a dilemma. But it was not one requiring him to declare the end of "big government." Within a year or two of becoming the unexpected president, his dilemma was between meeting the escalating costs of the Vietnam war and meeting the demands of racial justice and poverty. He tried to address both, and to do so without the major tax increases required. The dilemma soon came to be seen as the competition between guns and butter.

This dilemma, and his inability to resolve it, was to be Lyndon Johnson's undoing. But his contribution to a restored Democratic Party foundation for the twenty-first century rests in his commitment to the use of pragmatic, activist government tools to address unavoidable social conflicts. Neglect, reliance on "a thousand points of light," or promotion of "faith-based charities" would have virtually guaranteed the destruction of entire sections of the nation's major cities and the potential for prolonged racial violence. Further, those antigovernment shibboleths used to avoid responsibility would have denied several generations of black and Hispanic Americans any sense of opportunity or hope.

Sometimes in human history, especially in a mass democracy that considers itself to be based on equality and justice, tax cuts for the rich, trickle-down economics, and laissez-faire doctrines simply will not suffice. That is, they will not suffice unless one does not consider oneself part of a society, a nation, a community, or if one is satisfied to seek retreat and protection behind the walls of one's gated community guarded all about by a well-paid, highly trained, and powerfully armed private army.

Being a Democrat and thus burdened by the belief that we are, one way or the other, all in this together, Lyndon Johnson did not permit himself to consider that selfish, some might say cowardly, option of responsibility avoidance. Like its predecessor, the New Deal, the Great Society, with its war on poverty, made serious mistakes. One was to believe that middle-income, taxpaying Americans would tolerate cumbersome governmental bureaucracies constructed to help the poor with the same forbearance with which they tolerated those bureaucracies constructed to help *them* in a previous age. In a word, it was all right to have a large Social Security or Medicare administration, but it was much less acceptable to pay for large public housing projects or food-stamp programs or aid to dependent children, especially when stories of "waste, fraud, and abuse" entered the political currency and "welfare queens" were reported to be driving their Cadillacs to pick up their food stamps.

Lyndon Johnson was, if nothing else, politically astute, and he understood that the nation, not then being in the dire straits of a Depression, was not in the mood for a second Roosevelt regime. But racial strife and the breakdown of urban order required national attention. The business community, financial investors, urban property owners, and mainstream Republicans all acknowledged that attention must be paid and the federal government had to act. Rather than simply create massive new federal agencies, some of which arose in any case, the Johnson administration relied on a creative federalism—national grants to state and local governments, in many cases lumped under the catchall title of "community block grants"—to carry out the war on poverty. It would be an approach much relied upon by his successor, Richard Nixon, who labeled this devolutionary approach "the new federalism."

Whether "creative" or "new," the use of state and local governments to achieve national objectives had the distinct political advantage of keeping the size of "government," meaning the federal government, basically level, while state and local governments, those closest to the people, grew like Topsy. In this respect, President Clinton's declaration of the end of the era of "big government" came almost thirty years too late.

By purchasing racial and urban peace through major new national programs administered by state and local governments, Johnson refined the New Deal and adapted its experimental approach to an age where the minority poor, rather than the dispossessed middle class, required the nation's attention. The money would come from the federal government, but the administration would be carried out by states and municipalities.

The issue this raises for the Democratic Party in the twenty-first century is whether Lyndon Johnson's use of federal systems and structures to address national crises offers an additional pillar upon which to build a party platform for the future. However one answers that question, there is no denying the pillar that Johnson does provide: racial equality.

With the assassinations of John and Robert Kennedy, and more significantly of Martin Luther King Jr., the tenuous peace maintained by Lyndon Johnson between high-unemployment, crime-ridden, urban racial ghettos and the rest of the nation collapsed, and there were riots in the streets, multiple city blocks in multiple cities set afire, and the rise of fearsome Black Panther organizations. The thinness of society's veneer was revealed, and the Kerner Commission reported that the nation required large-scale new housing and employment initiatives and the removal of remaining barriers to opportunity for minority Americans. Four decades later Hurricane Katrina would blow the carefully constructed lid off racial and economic inequality in urban New Orleans.

Yet another generation of Americans would profess profound shock, and a conservative Republican president, heretofore dedicated to "faith-based charities," would commit the nation's government to correcting this inequality. Like the pitifully few blocks of ice available in the hurricane's aftermath, this commitment would dissolve virtually overnight in the heat of budget deficits, the costs of the war in Iraq, and the restoration of party orthodoxy opposed to social programs on the part of Republican congressional leaders.

In the case of civil rights, gender equality, and a wide variety of other progressive efforts to achieve equality and justice, there has been a pattern. Democrats have taken the lead, conservative Republicans have resisted, Democrats have received the political backlash from those opposed to racial and gender equality, and, after the political dust settles, Republicans accept and promote the social change as if it had been their idea in the first place. Little has been heard today from mainstream Republican conservatives about repealing civil rights laws or statutory protection of women's economic rights.

In the case of civil rights particularly and equal justice for all generally, Democrats must now reclaim their rightful heritage and, together with Roosevelt's ideal of social justice, Truman's alliance-based internationalism, and Kennedy's republican virtue, make equal justice a central feature of their twenty-first-century manifesto.

Liberalism, Centrist Minimalism, and the Restoration of the Enlightenment

Before the next Democratic Party renaissance, there must be much greater clarity about terms. Language and the meaning of words are often consciously confused, left vague, or purposely perverted to achieve a political objective. The Democratic Leadership Conference was formed following the defeat of the Democratic ticket in 1984. Its stated purpose was to "move the party to the center." This was to be achieved by focus on issues of concern to "ordinary people"—middle-class, middle-income Americans presumably uninterested in the Democratic Party's traditional liberal message. The "center" also was to be reached by abandonment of activist social concerns focused on the poor and reduction of the burden of regulations imposed by previous Democratic administrations and Congresses.

Unquestionably, repositioning the Democratic Party helped elect President Clinton a few years later, and he responded by acknowledging that "the era of big government is over," a phrase presumably meant to include much of the Democratic Party's domestic agenda from 1932 until 1968. It must be noted, however, that his election was also mightily helped by the third-party candidacy of Ross Perot in 1992, and by the traditional presumption in favor of incumbents and the technology boom in his reelection in 1996. The ideological implication of the new centrism, however, was the abandonment of the idea of liberalism, by then much under demonizing attack from a virulent and ubiquitous right wing.

The theory of the centrists seemed to be that if an entire state of mind, or outlook on life, comes under attack, then abandon it and, if need be, denounce it. Under such circumstances it is sometimes necessary to revisit what that outlook, that state of mind entails. According to most dictionaries, to be "liberal" is to be generous, to be open-minded, to be magnanimous and charitable, to be progressive and reform-minded, to be catholic, and perhaps most of all to be enlightened. Democratic Party leaders and elected officials will, of course, have to speak for themselves—and most of them have done so by proclaiming, even before accused, "I'm no liberal." Are they saying by this self-denunciation that they reject all those qualities that have traditionally characterized the liberal mind? If so, and particularly if they are doing so out of fear, this is not only cowardly, it is small-minded and foolish.

One is reminded of the old political story from the age of

Prohibition, another small-minded era in American history not unlike our own, that involves a political candidate's response to a stern question about his views on alcohol. "If you mean by liquor, Madam," the wily politician says, "demon rum, that destroyer of homes and ruin of families, that foul poison of the human mind," etc., "then I am against it. But," he quickly continues, "if you mean that elixir of the spirit, that stimulant of poetry and music, that liberator of the human mind," etc., "then, Madam, I am for it."

Despite the mindless right-wing rants and ditto-head demonization of "liberals," if most Democrats, or indeed most Americans, were to be asked if they would wish themselves to be characterized by the liberal qualities listed above, they would gladly accede. But, "if by 'liberal' you mean big government, giveaway programs, high taxes, confusing regulations, and overbearing bureaucrats," they would also quickly add, "then I'm no liberal." Where all can agree is that there is no danger of the right-wing fanatics now occupying the Republican Party soapboxes (on television and radio) ever being described as generous, open-minded, magnanimous, charitable, progressive, catholic, or, most especially, enlightened.

This is not necessarily an argument for resurrection of the word "liberal," though that would by no means be a bad thing. It is an argument for enlightened, tolerant, progressive, open-minded, generous Americans to restore these qualities both to the public dialogue and to government administration, call them what you will. If Democratic Party

leaders are reluctant or afraid to do so, then surely some political movement will arise with the necessary courage, hon-
esty, and magnanimity of spirit. A surprising, perhaps
stunning, number of us who wish to restore nobility to
America will flock to that movement.

Late-twentieth-century and early-twenty-first-century
America will not be seen by history as a particularly epic
time and place. It will certainly not be seen as a time of gen-
erosity of spirit, or liberation of the human mind, or bold
and creative world leadership, or of the renaissance of art
and culture. Records will be sifted by future historians in
search of explanations for the narrow, regressive, timid response on the part of American leaders, indeed for the absence of statecraft and of giant statesmanlike figures, at a
time when the Cold War ended and relative peace prevailed, globalization and information were bringing huge
new opportunities, nations adrift looked to the American
colossus for direction, and the world was poised for a new
age of progress, expansiveness, and enlightenment.

Where were the visionaries, the grand strategists, the
cloud-splitters, the large-souled leaders? Where were the
Roosevelts, Trumans, and Kennedys? Where were the Marshalls, Achesons, Harrimans, McCloys, and Kennans?

Instead, throughout much of this critical period, America, and thus much of the world, has been led by figures
who have lacked curiosity, rejected learning, refused to entertain even the notion of enlightenment, found physical

pursuits more rewarding than reading, were bored by international travel and exchange, lived in self-sustaining cocoons protected by those much like themselves, and even grandly permitted themselves to believe that they were—more or less—divinely inspired. Could there possibly be a connection between the rise of this pathetic, small-bore leadership and the demonization of liberalism, with all it has historically connoted?

The history of this curious detour in American history, this rule by tiny-minded right-wingers, will reveal that it represented not a rejection of twentieth-century liberalism but a rejection of the eighteenth-century Enlightenment—the very intellectual foundation of the American Republic.

President Bush has stated his reliance on divine, not human, guidance. He has revealed no particular personal interest in current events or history, little if any curiosity about foreign cultures, scant interest in scientific investigation or new breakthroughs in learning. He denies, in the face of surpassing scientific evidence, the destruction caused by climate change. If he invites scholars and thinkers to White House conversations, it is a very well kept secret. Thomas Jefferson believed in "the progress of the human mind," including the minds of presidents. George W. Bush seems content with divinely revealed but medieval truths.

Thus, the task facing the Democratic Party is not only to restore the authentic meaning and qualities of liberalism, but even more to reestablish on American soil and in the

American soul the essence of the Enlightenment, which made American democracy possible.

Such a task will require larger-bore leadership than has emerged in recent years. It will require men and women devoted to statesmanship. It will require the restoration of statecraft, the art and science of governance with a perspective on history. It will require an act of immense will to liberate ourselves from the small-minded, bitter, divisive politics of the day. We must pray for that renaissance. But since prayer is too precious to waste, and for the reasons to follow, that prayer should be directed mostly for the currently drifting Democratic Party.

4

THE HEDGEHOG AND THE FOX

An enterprise to restore American statesmanship and state-craft seems obvious enough, yet many people, especially those not actively involved in party politics, do not understand why it has not been done or is not being done. The answer to that question requires an understanding of the fundamental differences between the Republican and Democratic parties, their disparate structures, their contradictory outlooks on governance, and their widely diverse notions of the very nature of organized society and life itself.

An early Greek called Archilochus used the fable of the hedgehog and the fox to point out a basic difference between two kinds of people. The fox, he said, knows many things. The hedgehog knows one big thing.

It isn't clear whether Republican self-certainty is based

on the idea of preemptive warfare, tax cuts, or a global religious crusade. Nor is having only one, or three, big ideas a guarantee of achieving either truth or success. My late colleague Daniel Patrick Moynihan used to remind us of the British prime minister who had but one idea—and it was wrong.

Nevertheless, it is important to note that during the period of its ascendancy from 1932 to 1968, the Democratic Party had one big idea, and it was this: *The national government has a central and positive role to play in bettering the lives of all Americans.*

Since then, divisions within the party over Vietnam, civil rights for minorities and equal rights for women, when and where to use military force, environmental versus development interests, and a host of other controversies have fractured the Democrats' big idea and reduced us to a party of foxes. We know many things, but these disparate policies lack cohesion around one, or three, big ideas. Our pudding, to quote Churchill, lacks a theme.

In the interest of suggesting ideas to create that cohesiveness and coherence in the context of the revolutionary world of the early twenty-first century, I would like to propose three large purposes, deeply rooted in traditional Democratic ideals, that might offer the party a chance to recapture the best of its hedgehog past and provide a confused American nation a clearer sense once again of our principles and our virtues.

America has three historic tasks today: First, we must create new international structures to manage this revolutionary world; second, we must reestablish the principles of community and justice at home; and, third, we must restore the ideal of the American republic.

These tasks mirror the challenges faced by the great Democratic presidents—Roosevelt, Truman, Kennedy, and Johnson—in the twentieth century. Further, these goals can be undertaken *only* by the Democratic Party because they require a core belief in internationalism, in social cohesion, and in civic virtue—beliefs contrary to the predominant Republican ideology of the day.

Significantly also, achieving America's large purposes is not a particularly liberal undertaking, nor does it require the confusing tactical calculation so predominant in the 1990s of "moving to the center." Stabilizing a disordered world, achieving a just community, and restoring our republic are, in fact, profoundly conservative goals that can be achieved only through progressive means.

To begin, we must understand the world in which we live. Globalization and information are twin revolutions remaking the world's economy and challenging the authority of the nation-state. The idea of national sovereignty is becoming frayed. And the very nature of war and conflict is changing.

Taken all together, these radical transformations are challenging the viability and effectiveness of traditional economic structures and political institutions. Yet most political leaders of both parties try to govern as if nothing fundamental has changed.

Much of the discontent with democratic government these days can be traced to the disconnection between our traditional institutions and a host of new realities to which they are incapable of responding.

Consider these new realities: proliferation of weapons of mass destruction; the failure of states; the rise of nonstate actors; mass south-north migrations in Europe and North America; climate change and global warming; increased competition for global energy supplies; the threat of pandemics such as AIDS, avian flu, and other viruses; and, of course, terrorism itself.

All these new realities share two characteristics: They cannot be addressed by military means alone, and they cannot be solved by any individual nation, including our own. We should add a third characteristic: The existing international organizations are ill-equipped to deal with any of them. And politically, these new realities do not lend themselves to either liberal or conservative solutions.

If you agree with these observations, you are left with three choices: We can ignore the rest of the world and try to go it alone; we can continue to try to muddle through using international institutions created before or during the Cold War; or we can disenthrall ourselves and think anew.

Unilateralism is failing, in Iraq and elsewhere. Some

Cold War institutions, such as NATO, lack a current mission. And others, such as the UN itself, badly require fundamental restructuring. Therefore, we have no choice but to adopt the third course.

Thus, *America's first task is to lead the world in creating new institutions to collectively address these new global realities.*

By way of example, that means an international peacemaking force to prevent mass violence when states fail and ethnic and tribal wars arise. It means an international agency trained and equipped to manage failed states and carry out nation building to reduce mass migrations, genocide, and chaos. It means closely linking national public health services around the world not just to respond to viral pandemics but also to suppress them before they occur. It means establishing a global banking regulatory authority to prevent collapse of international financial networks. It means creating an international environmental regulatory authority to reduce adverse climate change and manage transition away from carbon fuels. It means creating a new international inspection authority to prevent proliferation of weapons of mass destruction.

These are but a few of the many new challenges facing America and the world in the twenty-first century. They are possibly no greater than, but most certainly different from, the problems facing our leaders at the end of World War II and the beginning of the Cold War.

Then, Franklin Roosevelt and Harry Truman presided over the creation of the United Nations, the North Atlantic Treaty Organization, the World Bank and International Monetary Fund, the Bretton Woods Agreement, the World Trade Organization, and a host of other institutions amounting to nothing less than a new world order. Though that phrase drives fringe groups mad, this is exactly what we did six decades ago in a totally different world, and it helped save democracy and preserve world peace. Given their unilateralist, antialliance stance, it is impossible to imagine today's neoconservative Republicans replicating anything like this leadership attitude for the United States, a stance and vision that helped make Franklin Roosevelt and Harry Truman great presidents, great world leaders, and historic figures.

Today we again face the challenge to remake and restructure a new and different world. This challenge is at the core of the global leadership required of a superpower, and it can be met only by the American political party most identified with internationalism then and now.

But this crucial step of recognizing a set of new realities and creating new institutions to deal with them, as both Roosevelt and Truman did, will not address the most crucial new reality here at home—and that is the loss of social cohesion, the sense of community, and the imperative of social justice.

From the time of the Great Depression through the 1960s, we established and maintained a consensus that served us well. It was based on the instinctive notion that we are all in this together, that we are a national community, that we all do better when the fewest are left behind. We may call this a community of justice because it recognizes that we are a fellowship of shared interests, a community, and that fairness and equality, the core of justice, are the basis of a civilized society.

Instead of this cohesive philosophy, for the past twenty-five years we have abandoned our national consensus and have replaced the principles of justice and community with notions of personal acquisition and autonomy and with the attitude that "we are all in this for ourselves and devil take the hindmost." While fighting the Cold War and moving beyond it into the new century, America has lost its sense of itself and who we are as a nation.

This attitude makes it easy to "support the troops" while not wanting one's own son to serve in the military. It permits us to declare "war on terrorism" without requiring private corporations to contribute by protecting themselves. It is a war for which we are not being asked to pay or sacrifice. It encourages the false faith that reducing the taxes of the wealthiest somehow helps those in the middle whose incomes are stagnant. It reverts to the primitive and disproved idea that the poor are poor by choice. And it conveniently substitutes private charity, "a thousand points of light" and "faith-based initiatives," for the principle of community responsibility.

America today has a fundamental choice to make. Will we continue to revert to the laissez-faire law of the jungle and of Darwinian social policy? Or will we recapture our ideal of community, of common interests and common concerns? This public crossroads cannot be avoided and it cannot be deferred. And if we reestablish the sense of a commonwealth or community commons, it can be implemented in practice only by the philosophy of the Democratic Party.

For we have, at least for the time, wrongly decided that individual opportunity requires abandoning the ideal of justice, that we cannot combine personal initiative with shared interest and community values. To follow this path further into the twenty-first century is to abandon the notion that America's national interest is something greater than acquiring oil supplies in the Persian Gulf.

If the ideal of a just community means anything at all, it must mean an equitable apportionment of tax burdens, a shared responsibility for our national defense and security, and accountability to future generations for our management of their resources. For, as Edmund Burke wrote concerning the ongoing community, it is "a partnership not only between those who are living, but between those who are living, those who are dead, and those who are to be born."

If the Democratic Party is to deserve the opportunity to lead America again, it must demonstrate a leadership inspired by its great twentieth-century presidents, by first and foremost recapturing the ideals of community and justice. The party must identify what we hold in common and promote both the cause of justice and the means of achieving our common good and common interests together.

The Republican Party is and will remain the party of individual and private interests. Democrats are obliged, therefore, to become once again the party of the common good, of community, and of justice for all. To fail in this task is to abandon our heritage and to become some ill-defined "centrist" party with no compass, no clear purpose, and little reason for existence.

The third and most important task is to restore the ideal of the American Republic. That ideal is founded on one central, powerful belief: that we must earn our rights by performance of our duties.

The twentieth century was a century of democratic rights, and rightly so. Because of the Democratic Party, minorities and women were finally, after civil war and domestic controversy, admitted to full citizenship, and our nation is greatly the better for it and is closer to living up to its democratic promise. But in the struggle for equal rights we lost sight of the notion of citizen duty, the central ideal of the ancient republic.

There is more to being an American than begrudgingly paying taxes and being conscripted in time of national peril. The duties of American citizenship include participation in the public life of the community and nation, attending public meetings, demonstrating concern for local and national governance, serving willingly on juries, learning about the issues of the day and engaging in enlightened discussions, supporting candidates, voting in elections, volunteering for community projects and encouraging others to do so, and most of all taking the duties of citizenship seriously.

Democracy is concerned with the *right* to vote. The republic is concerned with the *duty* to vote.

Too many Americans take their rights for granted simply because they neglect their duties. The great truth about America today is this: *We will never be a great democracy until we first become a great republic.*

The ideal of the republic, so treasured by our Founders, was based upon the sovereignty of the people, not powerful financial interests, and upon the vigilant resistance to corruption of our politics by those who place their special interests ahead of the common good and the common interest.

Alas, however, we as a nation do not participate; we surrender our sovereignty to powerful interests that corrupt our politics, and we too often place our own narrow concerns over those of the society and nation and the protection of our own personal rights ahead of the performance of our citizen duties.

By neglect of our civic virtues we diminish the very republic whose flag we salute. We do not honor our republic by saluting its flag and chanting convenient patriotic rhetoric. We honor our republic by performing our duties as citizens.

Our Founders did not talk of values. They talked of virtues. The virtues upon which they founded the American republic were civic involvement and citizen participation, the people's sovereignty—"power to the people," resistance to corruption by special interests, and preservation of a sense of the common good—what we would call our national interest.

The strength of our republic in the twenty-first century will be measured by our commitment to these virtues.

Few generations have faced the challenges and the opportunities that now confront us. We have entered the world of a new century that bears its own unaddressed realities. Are we creative enough—do we possess the imagination of the leaders of Harry Truman's time—to devise new cooperative institutions to address these challenges, as they did in their day?

We have drifted away from the ideal of a nation founded on justice. Do we have enough sense of community, of compassion, to pull together rather than to pull apart, to recapture the conscience of the people around the belief in the justice of the community as we did in Franklin Roosevelt's time and Lyndon Johnson's time?

We have pursued our individual rights at the expense of our civic duties. Are we courageous enough to accept responsibility for earning our rights by performance of our duties as John Kennedy, and Thomas Jefferson, believed we must?

These are the three great challenges that now confront

us. Can we reinvent the world? Can we return the powerful meaning of justice to the center of our society and nation? Can we restore the ideal of the republic that caused our Founders to pledge their lives, their fortunes, and their sacred honor?

The answer to these questions will largely determine the future of the Democratic Party, for only a restored Democratic Party can reawaken a national commitment to a community of justice, alliance-based internationalism, and a sense of republican virtue.

More important, the answer to these questions will determine what kind of nation we will be in the new century and what kind of America we will leave to our children. It is no easy task to remake and restore a great political party. There is no quick fix that any media advisers can produce. This task lies well beyond slogans and pieties, beyond glib references to our glorious past, even beyond elaborate fund-raising dinners. The hunger of the American people for their own party, uncorrupted by special interests and lobbyists, dedicated to the proposition that there is a genuine national interest, and led by women and men of courage and conviction, is profound.

To pursue the path of conviction and courage demands payment of a heavy price, especially for those who see political office as a career. It requires placing the pleas of interest groups second to the interests of the party and, even more important, to the interests of the country. It is the rare politician who is strong enough to say no to the pleas of a multitude of interest groups, all with campaign contributions in their hands, and to point them instead to their role in achieving the common good. But that is exactly the kind of politician many Americans now seek.

To re-create this Democratic Party requires rising above self-interest and political careerism, moving well beyond the desperation for power, and restoring our ancient national soul. This is no task for cowards or those whose convictions transiently emerge, then disappear. Nor is this merely a call for restoration of a political party. It is a call for restoration of a political party with strong convictions and the courage those convictions provide, a party whose unique heritage equips it for service to the nation in its hour of need.

If the Democratic Party rejects this call, it will have ensured its decline and eventual disappearance into the pages of history, like the Whigs of old, and it will be replaced by a new party that adopts the ancient ideals and spirit it has abandoned. If, however, the Democratic Party recovers the principles that once made it great and that earned it the public's approval to govern, it will then show the courage and conviction required to make America truly great in a new century.

PART TWO

LEADERSHIP
FOR THE
TWENTY-FIRST
CENTURY

5

CLIMBING OUT OF
THE BIG MUDDY

As this critique began by indicting the Democratic Party's leadership for supporting an unnecessary preemptive war in the Middle East, a detour caused as much as anything else by the party's detachment from its historic anchorage, so now we should propose a Democratic strategy to extricate the United States from an unwise and destructive occupation as the first step toward the party's renaissance.

Why the party's leaders have failed to band together to propose a plan for Iraqi disengagement, especially in the many months since the bases for the war have proved false and the occupation has turned disastrous, remains a great mystery even to those of us who have been active in the party for decades, to say nothing of rank-and-file party members, independents, and the public at large increasingly looking for an alternative to the blindly stubborn and unproductive Bush policy.

Despite the curious, and sad, reluctance of a number of Democratic Party leaders to propose means for liberating our nation from the Iraqi briar patch, there are constructive steps available to achieve that result, even as the Bush administration clings blindly to its "stay the course" rhetoric. The keys to liberating Iraq and liberating ourselves from Iraq are: know your enemy; divide and conquer; welcome help; create economic unity; and share burdens and rewards.

The fatal flaw in the Bush occupation is its insistence that all those attacking our troops and facilities are "terrorists." Any number of military and civilian analysts have consistently stated that we face two very distinctive opponents: national insurgents on the one hand, foreign jihadists on the other. Some estimates put the percentage of national insurgents at about 90 percent of all those resisting our occupation, which means the foreign jihadists represent 10 percent or even fewer. Numerically, insurgents are estimated at somewhere between twenty thousand and forty thousand, and jihadists are estimated at anywhere from five hundred to four thousand.

To understand the difference, one must ask this question: How many of these people simply want us out of their country, and how many people are going to follow us home when we eventually depart? The purpose of the national insurgents, largely Sunni Iraqi Arabs, is to get us to leave their country. The purpose of the foreign jihadists, including many Saudi Arabians, is to kill Americans wherever they can find us. By insisting that they are all "terrorists," President Bush guarantees that we will occupy Iraq at least as long as the British (or their surrogates) did—about thirty-five years. This is the "course" that he wishes us to "stay."

The first step in a new policy toward Iraq, then, is to drive a wedge between the national insurgents and the foreign jihadists by negotiating with the former to help eradicate the latter. We should more seriously negotiate with moderate Sunni Arabs, and there clearly are a large number, to establish an agreement for a mutual and speedy drawdown of forces. The United States would agree to a two-phased withdrawal whereby combat forces will be withdrawn from occupational roles to bases outside the cities in exchange for verifiable insurgent disarmament. Once insurgent disarmament is complete, the disengaged U.S. forces would then be withdrawn from the country on a unit-by-unit basis. Additionally, in response to insurgent disarmament, Sunnis would be guaranteed full political participation with protected civil and political rights.

As this mutual disengagement is taking place, the United States should obtain Sunni commitments to help in the isolation, suppression, and eradication of the foreign jihadist elements in Iraq. The Sunnis have tolerated their presence and made common cause with them in the shared hope of getting the Americans to leave. Once that is clearly happening, the Sunnis not only have no further use for the foreigners, they have a positive motive for removing them from Iraqi soil. Because they have been cooperating in the insurgency, the Sunnis will know the identity, location, and methods of the jihadists and will be crucial players in their eradication in ways that we can never hope to achieve on our own.

Iraqi nationalists, whether Sunni, Shiite, or Kurdish, will also want assurances that the United States intends no permanent military presence in Iraq. Thus, the United States should declare that it is not constructing and will not construct permanent military bases in Iraq. Some might wish to quibble over what is "permanent" and what is not. But clearly, pouring concrete foundations for barracks and welding steel for armories is permanent, whereas tents and trench latrines are not. We either intend to maintain a long-term military presence in Iraq—and there is little doubt that that was (and perhaps even today still is) the intent of the neoconservative policy makers in the Bush government, though it was never revealed as such to the American people—or we do not.

Though the American press corps has seemed strangely uninterested in this question—one that goes to the very heart of our intentions in starting the war in the first place—now is the time to find out. The latest evidence was that at least four, and possibly as many as a dozen, permanent military bases are being built throughout the country.

One predictable scenario for the neoconservatives is to arrange for the new government in Baghdad to invite American forces to stay in Iraq as a semipermanent, Korea-like stabilizing force and thus legitimize construction of several garrisons for the stay-behind forces. These may amount to troop levels of as many as fifty thousand on a rotating basis and would provide the legitimacy for a permanent U.S. military presence in the Middle East. Once again, the French and other colonial powers will testify to the vulnerability of static garrisons to a continuing anti-occupation insurgency.

A serious disengagement plan, however, must be based on a central reality: We cannot insist on a pro-American, client-state Iraqi government of the sort long envisioned by neoconservatives. This may have been their dream, but Iraq's long, complex history and complicated mixture of cultures should have shown it years ago to have been a pipe dream.

In any case, we will never end our self-defeating occupation and assure Iraqis and others in the volatile region of the Middle East that we have no imperial intentions, as they now widely suppose, until this issue is settled. It is one thing to continue intensive diplomatic and even commercial attention to the area; it is quite another to leave behind several brigades (or perhaps a full division or more), helicopter wings, and weapons depots. This issue will be the clearest indicator of our policy and intentions. Either we came to bring democracy to the Iraqis, or we came to use Iraq as the base from which we would wield our influence through military force far into the future.

Few would dispute now that the restoration of order, security, and stability in Iraq is going to take far longer than we were led to believe when the preemptive war was undertaken in 2003. "We can't simply walk away now" is the way this is usually put. Therefore, any serious disengagement plan must provide for replacement capabilities in training and equipping Iraqi security forces.

This is a role that NATO can fill, but our allies must be asked, because NATO nations are already providing more than sixteen thousand troops for stabilization and nation building in Afghanistan. NATO peacekeeping units can oversee the training of Iraqi police and military forces and move those trained units into the principal security roles, especially border control missions to seal Iraq off from foreign jihadists. Those jihadists in any case will have much less interest in Iraq once the United States has departed, and will be much less welcomed by Iraqi citizens.

Persuading NATO nations to assume this role will require diplomacy, especially since many of its member nations were peremptorily and arrogantly dismissed as "old Europe" (in the words of Secretary of Defense Donald Rumsfeld) when they refused to support the Bush administration's preemptive invasion. Nevertheless, skilled diplomats have overcome greater hurdles when they have a will to do so and when they can offer incentives. Further, NATO troops are filling important security and combat support roles in Afghanistan and are perfectly capable of training Iraqi security units.

The incentive for NATO and other democratic nations to participate in Iraq should be provided by internationalizing the country's reconstruction program. Construction and engineering companies from European and some Asian nations should be both permitted and encouraged to participate in competitive bidding for major infrastructure project contracts. Energy and electrical systems, water and waste treatment plants, transportation facilities, and communications projects should not be handed out to a few politically favored American companies.

Further, the burden of financing Iraq's reconstruction should not be borne solely by United States taxpayers. We should quickly establish a Bank for Iraqi Reconstruction financed by Western democratic governments. Given the ability of their own construction and engineering companies to participate in major reconstruction projects and thus to recycle the investment their national governments will make in this bank, this will provide the quid pro quo required by European and Asian countries to contribute. Faced with mounting reconstruction and occupation costs, President Bush appealed in the spring of 2004 both to NATO and to the Group of Eight nations to provide troops and financing for Iraq's reconstruction. He failed. He failed simply because he neglected to include the key component: He did not also invite those nations to bring their own major contractors into the economic distribution. His message was, "We want your money and your troops, but Halliburton will do all the work and reap all the profits."

Oil, of course, cannot be neglected. One of the Iraq war's many mysteries is the curious lack of discussion of oil production and distribution. A final piece in the plan to end United States occupation should be the creation of an Iraqi national oil company, composed of a consortium of the Iraqi Oil Ministry and major international producers, empowered by law to build modern petroleum production and distribution facilities with revenues fairly distributed by national law to all Iraqis. The charter of this national oil company, by establishing fair revenue-sharing allocations, will go very far in allaying the fears of Sunnis and other minorities that oil wealth will be divided between the Shiites and the Kurds, on whose territories most of the oil resources are located.

These elements of an occupation-ending policy—know your enemy, divide and conquer, welcome help, create economic unity, and share burdens and rewards—are complementary and self-reinforcing. By dividing national insurgents from jihadists, we have much greater hope of ending the insurgency and crushing the jihadists. By negotiating mutual disarmament between national insurgents and the U.S. military, we have much greater hope of sharply reducing violence and bringing the Sunnis into the political mainstream. By declaring that the United States plans no permanent military presence, we clarify American intentions to the Iraqi people, to the American people, and to the world. By making NATO the bridge between the U.S. occupiers and permanent Iraqi security capabilities, we defuse anger and violence against the United States. By engaging broad-based Western financing and construction capabilities, we sharply reduce the financial burdens on the U.S. Treasury and share both burdens and rewards of reconstruction. And by establishing an Iraqi national oil production and revenue-sharing entity, we eliminate the accusation that the United States invaded Iraq for its oil, and we guarantee that all Iraqis will share in its benefits.

Obviously, many other pieces and nuances can be added to this policy outline. It is offered here not as a definitive solution but to demonstrate that alternatives exist to the destructive "stay the course" rhetoric. It is meant further to be proof to a strangely silent Democratic leadership that constructing an opposition party plan for Iraq is not, in the currency of the day, "rocket science."

As distracting as Iraq has become—unnecessarily, to my mind—it cannot be permitted to prevent our current administration from addressing a host of even greater challenges swiftly and often silently around us. Future generations of Americans must learn from both the Vietnam and

Iraq experiences that the American superpower must not permit itself to become so obsessed with one crusade that it neglects its global responsibilities. While we slog through the Big Muddy of Iraq, large-scale events are transpiring across the planet that desperately call for our attention.

6

THE NEGLECTED WORLD
BEYOND IRAQ

There are many reasons why history will judge the expedition to Iraq to have been folly—false premises and false justification; a total lack of reconstruction planning; the complete misreading of the political structure and ignorance of a complex national culture and history; a huge underestimation of the financial costs; the failure to anticipate the insurgency; the exhaustion of the U.S. Army, Marine Corps, National Guard and Reserves; catastrophic casualties—and the consequences continue. To this sad tribute to arrogance must be added the distraction of the United States from its larger mission in the world.

As America bleeds and is bled in Iraq for the fourth straight year, it is not single-mindedly pursuing the real war on terrorism. It is not pursuing a vitally necessary energy security policy. It is not creating an effective homeland security system. It is not recapitalizing its education system, the centerpiece of its true national security. It is not reorganizing its twentieth-century alliances to meet new twenty-first-century realities. It is refusing to participate in collective efforts to address climate change and global warming. It is not reforming and restructuring its military forces for an age in which the nature of warfare and conflict is dramatically changing. Its obsession with Saddam Hussein and Iraq has distracted the United States from true world leadership at a time of vital change.

It is as if Thomas Jefferson had permitted himself to be so distracted by the Barbary pirates in 1803 that he totally neglected the historic and complex diplomatic negotiations with the British, French, and Spanish. But of course Jefferson could grasp more than one thought at a time.

The Clinton policy of "enlargement" and "engagement" sought to convert the Cold War policy of containment, carried out mainly through military vigilance and presence, to a more benign, less confrontational global presence, encouraging democracy, promoting development, and fashioning collective security measures. This approach, albeit ad hoc especially in the security arena, avoided previous American postwar tendencies toward withdrawal and isolation from a turbulent world. To recall once again the memorable Churchillian observation, this foreign policy pudding had no theme. It was difficult to find the large purposes that defined "enlargement," purposes required of a superpower's grand strategy, and to find the consistent methods of applying America's powers, the patterns of "engagement," necessary to achieve those purposes. It was more often a case of us reacting to the world rather than the world reacting to us.

Few would claim that George W. Bush came to the presidency in January 2001 with a strategic sense of the role America ought to play in the twenty-first century. There had been, of course, pronouncements throughout the 1990s by prominent neoconservative thinkers that as the sole superpower, the United States ought to lay down the law and dictate terms for behavior in the Middle East, to condition China's ambitions, to return the Russian bear to its cage and keep it there, and to impose a "new world order" wherein America was top cop, benign dictator, and global enforcer. Little of this made its way into 2000 campaign rhetoric for the obvious reasons that it supposed an imperial role for America requiring the deployment of far-flung military forces, the expenditure of vast amounts of money, the administration of unstable governments, the reconstruction of failed states, and, perhaps most of all, the imposition of our will, at least as defined by the neoconservatives, on much of the rest of the world.

This vision, if one wishes to call it that, had the distinct disadvantage of loosening the American ship of state from its historical moorings and launching it on a course marked out by Rome, Spain, Great Britain, Germany, and a long series of other wrecked empires of history.

Needless to say, 9/11 and the subsequent war on terrorism gave the neoconservatives' vision its raison d'être. Here I find myself at distinct cross purposes with the preeminent Cold War scholar, John Lewis Gaddis, who has placed George W. Bush, together with Franklin Delano Roosevelt and John Quincy Adams, in the pantheon of American grand strategists. It must be said in his defense that Professor Gaddis rendered this sweeping judgment when the neoconservative scheme to remake the Middle East still had at least a theoretical chance of success. Even so, to portray George W. Bush as a grand strategist, particularly at the height of what was a chancy war at best, requires a flight of imagination and prognostication far exceeding my own capacity.

Nevertheless, the Bush administration's pursuit of the neoconservative vision in the Middle East has absolutely precluded another agenda, one markedly nonimperial, internationalist, multilateral, and coalition-based. That alternative vision required organizing the world community, probably through a new set of international institutions, to address the concerns of the commons—mass south-north migration, climate change, the spread of weapons of mass destruction and the technologies required to produce them, pandemics such as avian flu and AIDS, failed and failing states, and the struggle of more than three billion people for mere survival.

Such a vision, alas, was never adopted or convincingly promoted by the Democratic Party as a coherent alternative to the imperialist neoconservative agenda being pursued under the cover of the "war on terrorism." For reasons only history can provide, the Democratic Party, once the fountain of creative internationalism, turned out to be a fountain gone dry.

The sad truth, however, is that neither vision, that of the American imperium or that of America as organizer of the global commons, can be carried out without a major reorganization of our own priorities at home. U.S. world leadership, whether militant or benign, requires a productive economic base founded on superiority in scientific and technological education.

Building and preserving such a base requires a shift of economic priorities from consumption and debt to production, savings, and investment. We have gone in exactly the opposite direction during the George W. Bush years. A sound economic base requires an energy security policy. Instead, we are increasing our dependence on oil imports. It requires public consensus on national health care and pension security. Progress has been made on neither front. It requires recapitalization of our public and private research facilities. Instead, a network that provided technological superiority during the Cold War has been permitted to deteriorate and decline. This list of neglect by a Republican president and Congress is long. Yet once again, there has been no comprehensive Democratic plan to address and reverse it.

It would require little other than imagination and creativity for the Democratic Party to describe a new and more positive role for America in the world and to link that role to the serious, perhaps desperate, need for national renewal. Yet it has not happened. Over and over, visible Democrats such as myself continue to be asked by fellow citizens on the streets of our country's cities, "What do the Democrats stand for and when are they going to start speaking out?"

For the first few years of the twenty-first century the United States has pursued a libertarian, tax-cut-based economic policy at home that guarantees the following outcomes: Public investment in America's intellectual and physical infrastructure will not occur; a foreign policy based on preemptive warfare and unilateral intervention will continue; and a divisive domestic agenda dictated by the religious right will be pursued. All this at a crucial moment in history when a virtually opposite course should be taken. The duty of the Democrats, as the opposition party, is not simply to oppose but to *propose,* to put forward ideas to restore America at home and to set it on a constructive course abroad in the form of a grand strategy for the United States for the next quarter century.

Asked to explain the passivity, caution, and drift of my party, one must conclude that this enterprise will not take place without a consensus within the Democratic Party on an identifying set of principles, especially the principles established by the dominant Democratic leaders during eras of national triumph and success. Not until the Democratic Party has a principled base, accepted across its leadership and membership, will it be able to build upon that base a coherent domestic agenda and an international mandate that will be persuasive enough to earn majority support.

Constructing that base of principles and forming widespread consensus around it are formidable tasks for the party's leadership. Rank-and-file Democrats are looking for a leader who can and will undertake this task, and yet the early signs of the contest for party leadership and nomination for national office are not encouraging. Potential candidates are, predictably, raising immense amounts of money and trying to impress people with this achievement, contesting for the well-known media consultants and pollsters, recruiting organizers, building national organizations, seeking endorsements from interest groups, and generally behaving in traditional fashion.

But they are not doing the most important task—defining the Democratic Party's principles and core beliefs. They are not doing so for two reasons: Either they do not know how or they are afraid of alienating potential contributors or constituency groups who might wish to quarrel with those principles. Better to be vague and inclusive, goes the logic, than to be definitive and potentially exclusive. But this is the central reason for the failure of leadership, for the sense that conviction is absent, that courage is lacking. Those seeking to lead the party and nation cannot have it

THE COURAGE OF OUR CONVICTIONS

both ways. It is impossible both to coddle an amorphous and easy consensus and to demonstrate strength, conviction, and courage.

The 2008 Democratic presidential aspirants might be amazed by the multiple numbers of discouraged supporters they might activate for every narrow-minded, single-issue, special-interest member they might alienate if they took up the leadership task of saying, in bold, definitive, and categorical terms, exactly what the Democratic Party should stand for.

Only when we lay a firm base for the security of the livelihood of Americans will we be able to vigorously define America's role in the twenty-first-century world. This is not an easy task, because there is a great struggle between the two U.S. political parties for the high ground in defining that role, and that struggle has twisted our foreign policy into a pretzel. During much of the Cold War, Republicans defined themselves as foreign policy realists. They claimed to understand the world of superpower politics and to possess the diplomatic skills and military understanding to promote the interests of the United States in this world of power politics. Meanwhile, Democrats gradually became the peace party, the party that shrank from power and deplored violence. Democrats focused on economic development in the third world while Republicans focused on power politics in the first and second worlds.

Of course, these are gross overgeneralizations. The differences were not so stark and were often played out on the margins of foreign policy decision making. But toward the end of the twentieth century, and particularly after the end of the Cold War, Republican neoconservatives transformed themselves into the party of idealism, of bringing democracy to the world of dictators, of liberating oppressed peoples, of remaking the world in our image (whether it wanted to be remade or not). Witnessing this image transformation, Democrats became uncomfortable on two levels—with an aggressive foreign policy based on missionary zeal, and particularly with one that claimed the moral high ground. Here was a new thing, at least new since the Spanish-American War. We were now free to save the world, even if it required suppressing insurgencies resistant to our politics and our culture.

One analyst of the public mood reached this conclusion regarding the fine balance between pragmatism and moral idealism in late 2005:

> Currently, the scales are heavily tipped toward the moral component. The actively religious U.S. public tends to see the world in terms of good and evil, hold its own values in the highest moral esteem, and feel ready to make whatever sacrifices are required to combat what they perceive as evil. . . . He [President Bush] is on the side of good, and therefore what he says is right. The religiously committed will make whatever sacrifices he says are needed to protect the nation. Their sentiments echo the traditional theme of American exceptionalism: Americans are a people chosen for a special mission in the world and especially blessed by God.

Though these reflections have specifically to do with the Bush administration's political base in the evangelical South, they also illustrate the challenge for the Democratic Party in defining America's role in the world. If those currently in power see the world in terms of good and evil, and we are "on the side of good," then what other alternatives does that leave?

The Democratic alternative is first to point out that empire is empire even if undertaken for the most noble of motives and that America, like all other powers in history, cannot be both empire and republic. Additionally, Americans must be reminded that our Founders abhorred the notion of crusades. John Quincy Adams famously said that America "goes not abroad in search of monsters to destroy." Does that mean our Founders could not have comprehended George W. Bush's vision of a world made in our image? No, they could not have. The idea would have appalled them.

Finally, we are not merely exporting democracy to regions with no history of democracy; we are also exporting our popular culture, our commercial and material values, and our way of life (and many see us exporting as well those religious values that assert that we are good and those who oppose us are evil) to regions with their own history and their own cultures, which they do not wish to see overthrown by Americans armed with the weapons of the future.

A twenty-first-century Democratic foreign policy will be based on the ideas of alliance, cooperation, shared values and purposes within the context of individual national interests, shared security burdens, common economic interests, and a common interest in a peaceful world. Though we have cooperatively defeated imperialism, fascism, and communism, the United States was not created to stamp out evil in the world. We were not created to be the world's avenging angel. As politically convenient as it is for President Bush to proclaim himself and his nation as God's agents, we have a long way to go before we deserve such a divine mission.

An American crusade against evil can lead only to more imperial ventures, more occupations, more insurgencies, and the decline of our republic. It is well that we are not really serious about this or we would be in the same spot as we are in Iraq, if not worse, in North Korea, Iran, Syria, and a host of other countries.

7

TWENTIETH-CENTURY PRINCIPLES IN A TWENTY-FIRST-CENTURY WORLD

Policies must be devised for the realities of the times. Principles, on the other hand, are timeless. To the extent that policies deal with new realities through the application of timeless principles, they will have a good chance of success. The principles unique to the Democratic Party are commitment to social justice, alliance-based internationalism, civic duty, and equality for all. Those principles, and the policies based upon them by four Democratic presidents, established the identity of the modern Democratic Party. How might they apply to the realities we face today?

Franklin Roosevelt is most remembered for the New Deal, a scattershot approach to a myriad of Depression-era economic woes that was nevertheless remarkably cohesive, and for his leadership through World War II. The central principle of the New Deal was social justice, a sense that we were all in this together and that through our elected government we could unite to help each other out of hardship. Many in the wealthy upper class opposed this principle as socialist.

Yet out of the New Deal came a social safety net for the middle class and a ladder of opportunity for working people. Justice came to be defined in economic, not simply legal, terms. To have a degree of security in old age was a matter of justice. To have a right to bargain collectively for wages was a matter of justice. To be spared the indignity of poverty was a matter of justice. To have support in saving the family farm was a matter of justice. The real Roosevelt revolution was to expand the ideal of justice in the modern age.

The second revolution of the Roosevelt age was to regulate markets. Financial buccaneers had previously treated the American economy as an arena for unbridled speculation, manipulation, plunder, and rampant greed. By their excess they had exacerbated the Depression and driven most of the country into social and personal catastrophe. The "malefactors of great wealth," Theodore Roosevelt's term for them, were saved from their own excesses by market regulations guaranteeing genuine competition, transparency, and fair play. They did not like it then, and as with the New Deal's commitment to social justice, they have not liked it since.

Every conservative swing of the political pendulum for

the past seventy-five years has featured efforts at starving "big government," a persistent and negative euphemism for social justice and regulation of markets. And with those pendulum swings we have witnessed the inevitable rise of poverty and the reemergence of the financial buccaneers, never far below the surface of the marketplace. It was imminently predictable that, following a twenty-five-year age of market deregulation, first under Ronald Reagan, then the first George Bush, then the Republican-led Congresses of the 1990s, and finally the current President Bush, there would be a return of corporate corruption embodied by the Enrons, WorldComs, Tycos, and Qwests, among many others.

It was equally predictable, based on history, that an era of corporate excess would be accompanied by a spillover of graft into the halls of Congress itself—the gilded yachts of Jack Abramoff and a host of pirate bands cruising the Potomac dredging for political bottom-feeders.

For the Democrats it has been too tempting, during these pendulum swings to the right, to accommodate to the perceived public mood and the financial pressures against fair taxation and market regulation, to become "centrist," instead of using these periods of conservatism to remind the nation at large, and each new generation, of the cost of retreat to the age of laissez-faire, privatization, and every man for himself and devil take the hindmost. And the costs are always the same: poverty among children, marginalization of the elderly, and a parade of "perp-walking" buccaneers.

Having convictions, and the courage to express them when they may be unpopular, requires qualities that do not come naturally to the politician, especially the career politician. Pressures for conformity always outweigh the silent rewards of conviction. For the past three or more decades, taking up the cause of the impoverished has required both conviction and courage. Few Democratic voices have been heard. Thus the Rooseveltian heritage of social justice has been quietly abandoned, its principles expediently shelved, perhaps until the next great depression.

Yet those principles have a moral as well as a political dimension. Either it is the duty of a civilized society to care for its poor or it is not. There was a time when the Democratic Party said that it was. Either the Democrats no longer believe we have that duty, or we have abandoned those principles in the interest of achieving a degree of acceptability at a time when championing our duty to the poor is unpopular.

It is a pity that no means exist to require political parties to state their principles. It is expedient not to do so because such an exercise might drive voters away who find cause for disagreement. On the other hand, to restate clearly a commitment to social justice would go far to answer the definitional question: What do the Democrats stand for?

The best political advice I ever received came from the late Mike Mansfield, then the Senate majority leader. Shortly after I arrived in the Senate, he took the occasion to invite me aside and he said: "Draw a line. Fix a point beyond which you will not go and stick to it." Though his words were subject to some interpretation, it seemed clear to me that he was saying that there are principles more important than a political career.

The twentieth-century Democratic Party has always been more than an instrument for achieving power and providing a platform for personal political ambition. It had, at least in the past, a soul. It stood for something. It was based on certain principles. It was those principles that made it the dominant political force in America in the last century. It should be worth some consideration that when the Democratic Party began to separate itself from those principles, its authority and majority position eroded.

Ambiguity, the favorite hiding place for uncertain politicians, has its own dangers. One of the most often heard observations on America's main streets is, "I don't always agree with him (or her), but I know where he (or she) stands." Conviction offers its own rewards. It is worth the gamble to sacrifice the votes of those who may oppose concern for children, the elderly, and the poor in order to earn the votes of those looking for a party with conviction based on principle and the courage to stake out a moral stance.

Obviously, the most recent Democratic administration, saddled with recalcitrant Republican Congresses, favored "social programs" more than Republicans have. But since the decline of the Great Society there has been very little effort to focus public attention on the hard-core poor and to promote ideas to extend middle-class entitlement policies to the poorest among us. Republicans have salved their consciences by reliance on such slogans as "a thousand points of light" and "faith-based charities," even when it is transparently obvious that all the charity in America cannot alleviate the plight of the structurally poor and especially those too young, too old, or too infirm to work.

But social justice is not just for those in poverty or the working poor. The incomes, and therefore the standard of living, of middle-class Americans have been stagnant since the 1970s. Those trained and experienced in high-technology jobs benefited at least for a time during the economic bubble of the 1990s. A few even became millionaires. But these were rare. The life of most middle-income people has been characterized by two working parents, borrowing to finance college educations, credit card debt, large mortgages, and low savings rates. Even while the American economy seems the envy of the world, and while most Americans live better than the vast majority of humanity, life in the middle of our society is constantly threatened by failed pension plans, uncertain health care protection, downsized incomes caused by failed employers, and uncertainty in retirement years.

Social justice in the twenty-first century represents a different challenge than recovery from the Great Depression. As a society we must now acknowledge and protect pension rights, along with the human entitlement to decent health care, protection against corporate fraud, a clean environment, secure borders, a sound dollar, and confidence in government. These are not unreasonable or unachievable goals for a just society or a progressive, productive, and privileged nation. Justice is the principle—not just legal justice, but economic and social justice. As security now requires a broader understanding given the new realities we face, so Democrats must attend to a broader definition of social justice at a time when there are still unacceptable levels of poverty in America and when tens of millions of middle Americans are experiencing deep injustices in their country. Genuine justice must be a matter of principle.

Thus the first step for creating a new Democratic century is to restate the party's commitment to the principle of social justice and the ideal that no American should be left behind or victimized by unfairness in the national economy.

A second step would be for the Democrats to reclaim Harry Truman's principle of international alliance. Arguably, America's standing in the world is lower today than at any time in at least a century (with the possible exception of the Vietnam war era). International disdain has little or nothing to do with the "war on terrorism," which virtually all of our traditional allies support. It has to do with the unilateralism of preventive invasion, the disregard of international opinion, the casual dismissal of alliances that won two world wars and the Cold War, and an arrogance of power demonstrated only by the empires of history.

Harry Truman instinctively grasped two great truths in 1945: first, that America could not return to its prewar isolation, and second, that engagement in the world required strong friends and steadfast allies. The United States had joined an existing European alliance against German aggression in World War I and reluctantly entered World War II to help save Britain and to retaliate against Japan. Truman, and some very intelligent statesmen around him, thought it best to anticipate an expansionist Soviet Union and build alliances in anticipation of, rather than in reaction to, aggression.

Truman also recognized that it was as important to build economic security as it was to build military might. Indeed, our Western European allies, as well as our World War II enemies, could not afford to participate in cooperative and collective military security without a modern industrial base and expanding economy. Together with Secretary of State George Marshall and advisers like John J. McCloy, Averell Harriman, and others, Truman knew also that the new alliances had to include our rebuilt and democratized former enemies, Germany and Japan.

With the invasion of Iraq, the United States effectively undercut the rationale behind this fifty-five-year alliance upon which our security rested. And it did so with a remarkable and gratuitous demonstration of disdain, referring to that alliance as "old Europe." The Bush administration decided, for reasons that can only have been based on arrogance rather than intelligent calculation, to go it alone. If this self-destructive step advances America's national security in any measurable way, that has yet to be explained. In fact, there is no way it can be.

The isolationist Republican Party has returned to its historic roots, but with a big difference. It has managed to isolate the United States from the allies critical to our safety and success and has, at the same time, sent a powerful signal that we will undertake unilateral military action wherever and whenever we see fit. The United States will be engaged in the world, according to this theory, but only on our terms: We will use our power when, where, and how we like regardless of its effect on anyone else. The headline is "U.S. to Allies: Drop Dead."

It is imperative now that the Democratic Party restore the Truman principle of international alliance. If for no other reason, the struggle to suppress jihadist terrorism demands it. The center of radical Islamic jihad is not solely in the Middle East; it is in Europe as well, where alienated Muslim youths are especially susceptible to the radical ideology of al Qaeda and other groups. It will prove impossible for the United States to defend itself against the international jihad without maintaining a close integration of Western intelligence agencies, secret services, and special forces. And these are the agencies, services, and forces whose governments we have ridiculed and alienated. It may have provided some emotional gratification to Bush administration officials to have mocked our traditional European allies, but by no stretch of imagination did it advance the cause of American security.

The Truman alliance principle is even more relevant in the age of globalization. With the information revolution, global finance is pulling national economies closer together. To separate the United States from the democratic world is nothing less than an act of folly. Both major American political parties now advocate an international role for the United States, but with great differences in purpose and practice. For neoconservative Republicans, that role is focused on the Middle East and Asia, it features the use of military power, and it is unilateral. This policy (it is not a strategy) seeks to avoid the imperial label by claiming to export democracy rather than, as with the British empire, mere Western civilization.

The difference between the parties and their philosophies is whether one sees the world as dividing or integrating. For the Republicans, the world is dividing between a U.S.-defined democratic civilization and chaos. According to this theory, we must therefore bring as much of the Middle East—and its oil—as we can into our orbit and otherwise, except to confront potential competitors such as China, pull up the drawbridge. Former allies, particularly including "old Europe," have a choice of either following along or being left to their own devices.

Democrats generally believe in the continuation of our

traditional alliances and see the world as becoming more integrated through trade and information. But our party has yet to make the restoration of traditional alliances and the formation of new ones a centerpiece of a Democratic Party renaissance. We must do so, both to counter the notion that our foreign policy pudding has no theme and to offer to the American people and the world a much more constructive alternative to divisive unilateralism.

We no longer confront the possibility of communist expansion. We do confront metastasizing jihad, failed states, and the clash of cultures. We need the help of other democratic nations in addressing all three. We Democrats, being committed to international alliance, must promote a new age of cooperation mirroring that of 1946–47. We need a new (or redesigned) NATO, one collectively organized against jihadism, equipped to bolster failing states, and designed to bridge the gaps of cultural, social, and religious confrontation.

This kind of thinking has yet to characterize the Democratic Party today. In part this is the result of the failure of a new generation of statesmen and stateswomen, like those of the Truman era, to emerge. Given the critical need for such statesmanship, it is confounding that a phalanx of big-scale, large-thinking, experienced internationalists has not come forward. Part of the reason is the demonization of government and denigration of public service so popular over the past quarter century. But driving the most qualified people in our country out of national service is the surest way to guarantee the triumph of mediocrity, inexperience, and narrow bias in foreign policy formulation. It also contributes demonstrably to national insecurity.

Social justice and international alliance, the principles of Roosevelt and Truman, are key elements of a Democratic renaissance. But other principles, from John Kennedy and Lyndon Johnson, are equally important. With the exception of military service and during reformist eras such as the progressive movement, American citizens have rarely been challenged, by either party, to participate in public affairs and public life. John Kennedy restored the republican ideal to twentieth-century America. But that restoration faded with his death. A third principle constituting a Democratic Party foundation in the twenty-first century, then, is to resurrect the theme of citizen duty, participation, and empowerment.

Why is this important? Because forty years marked by assassinations, Watergate, deceptions over Vietnam and Iraq, astronomical campaign expenditures, and lobbyist scandals and corruption have all eroded citizen confidence in government and created the notion that there is nothing a citizen can do to change things. As a party that fundamentally distrusts government, Republicans cannot restore republicanism, the sense that all of us are responsible for governing our society. That task must fall to the Democrats.

There are, of course, many ways to contribute to society.

But the republicans of ancient times insisted that citizens, as central to their very status as citizens and as their duty, participate in government and in the decisions that affected their collective lives. Given today's Republican Party philosophy of autonomy and self-interest, only the Democratic Party can restore the ideal of the republic.

And it is an ideal with extremely important practical implications. The U.S. Commission on National Security for the 21st Century reported in 2001 that our nation's security was jeopardized by the declining caliber and quality of those willing to enter public service. After a quarter century of denigration of government, and the rise of an intrusive press, it is not surprising that the best citizens find things other than public service to do.

Each of us must make his or her own choices in this regard. But the National Security Commission found that our very security is in jeopardy because the most competent citizens in our nation have decided to do things other than serve their country. Perhaps no more vivid illustration of this principle exists in recent years than the performance of the head of the Federal Emergency Management Agency, Michael Brown, a political appointee almost totally unequipped to carry out his duties, during the aftermath of Hurricane Katrina. When unqualified people run the government, our government is ineffective, citizens lose confidence in their government, and the entire nation suffers.

Civic duty is a principle that resonates, especially with

young people. One has only to know about projects such as City Year, the forerunner of Americorps, to appreciate the responsiveness of young people to a noble challenge. City Year engages hundreds of young people in a number of cities every year in important community improvement projects and thus develops their sense of citizen duty and participation. Is there a doubt that a citizen engaged in civic life is also a better citizen? This principle is not only important to the Democratic Party, it is even more important to the nation as a means of empowering individual citizens and communities in the public life of their country.

As a lifelong advocate of some form of voluntary national service program for the young, or even midcareer or retired, citizens of the United States, I believe the call to civic duty will resonate as clearly today as it did for my generation in the early 1960s. We simply need Democrats with the courage of their convictions, including the conviction that we should all contribute to our nation's public life and future, to issue that call.

Republicans cannot advocate social justice because they are against the idea of a social safety net. Republicans cannot advocate international alliance because, at least currently, they are led by unilateral interventionists. Republicans cannot advocate civic duty because they are opposed to activist government.

These are principles that only the Democratic Party can advocate, and it *must* do so as a foundation and as guideposts for domestic and foreign policy. And these principles must expand to the fourth principle of a Democratic manifesto: equality, promoted by a string of Democratic presidents but raised to a moral level, in the form of civil rights for all citizens, by Lyndon Johnson.

Though he is identified most immediately with the prosecution of the Vietnam war, Johnson's greatest contribution was to establish the era of civil rights and to do so by changing the laws of the United States. Voting rights, housing rights, employment rights, equal access to public education, and the rule of law applied without regard to race all characterized the second half of the 1960s through statute and judicial decision. The plague of slavery, the central paradox of the nation's founding, so responsible for the bloody Civil War, so immediate to the American culture for more than a century thereafter, came finally to its legal end in the Johnson era.

The political irony, of course, is that it took a Southern president, and a Democrat, to cause this to happen. It had been the abolitionist wing of the Republican Party and a moderate Republican president, Abraham Lincoln, that had been most identified with the end of slavery. But the cause of civil rights began to emerge as a liberal Democratic issue for mid-twentieth-century leaders such as Eleanor Roosevelt, A. Philip Randolph, and Hubert Humphrey. Doing what was both right and long overdue had its price. Coming on the heels of Johnson's civil rights revolution, Richard

Nixon skillfully took political advantage of white anger in the South and converted the solid Democratic South to a Republican stronghold. Politics is particularly savory for those with a taste for irony.

But equality has many faces—economic, political, racial, and gender-based. Equality is a goal and an ideal. It is never perfectly reached. But ethical societies never cease to try. Because the Republican Party sacrificed its moral authority on the issue of civil rights for political advantage, the Democratic Party must restore the Johnsonian ideal, be the party of equality for all, and make that ideal a central principle in its twenty-first-century foundation.

What then *should* the Democrats stand for? We stand today, as we did in the previous century, for social justice, for international alliance, for civic duty, and for equality for all. These are the fundamental principles—values, if you will— that define the Democratic Party.

They are not policies. But if you accept these principles, then policies must and will emanate from them. Does a tax cut favor the rich? Then it must be opposed as incompatible with social justice and, where economically appropriate, replaced with tax cuts for the middle class and the working poor. Do those tax cuts create long-term deficits? Then they must be opposed as unjust to future generations. Do budget cuts, required to reduce deficits, fall most heavily on the poor and dependent young and elderly? Then they must be opposed on the same grounds. The positive side of this coin requires taxing and spending priorities that are fair and just to the greatest number, regardless of whether the beneficiaries possess wealth and power.

Is a trade policy protectionist? Then it erodes international alliances. Do dubious military interventions require the mockery of traditional allies? Then they are clearly unwise. Given a choice between unilateral action and collective action, do we unnecessarily choose unilateralism? Then that choice destroys alliance trust. Do we reject participation in international efforts to reduce climate change and establish international systems of justice? Then we further isolate ourselves from an increasingly integrated world community and endanger the planet and all its inhabitants. Contrariwise, policies based on principles of international integration, cooperation, and alliance have the greatest chance of continuing U.S. leadership, making the world safer, and making us more secure.

Does political rhetoric discourage citizen participation by featuring the government as adversary? Then it must be countered by a positive message that government is rightly the instrument of progress and citizen empowerment. Are young people told to disdain public service and focus on moneymaking? Then the Democrats must remind the country that we have public as well as private responsibilities. Are people led to believe that security can be found only in a gated community? Then they must be told that security cannot be privatized. Democrats should remind the nation that the citizen-soldier, today's National Guard, is the constitutional backbone of homeland security and must not be abused or stretched thin in foreign adventures.

Does public policy favor the rich and the white? Democrats must stand for the principle of equality for all. Are subtle (and not so subtle) campaign messages fashioned to appeal to racism? They must be denounced. Are favored groups, most of whom have made large campaign contributions, given special access to the corridors of power? We must wage a continuing fight against privilege and favoritism. It is the duty of Democrats to raise the flag of equality and justice in a nation occasionally prone to forget these principles.

Policies detached from principles become merely expedient. A party's platform comes to resemble, as have most recent Democratic platforms, a mere smorgasbord of special interest provisions, unrelated to each other or to any thematic foundation. The impression is then given, often too accurately, that the Democratic Party is simply a vehicle for individual political careers, the acquisition of power, and the satisfaction of ever-shifting, ever-changing coalitions of interest groups. Without a manifesto of principles, one with resonance in its rich history, the Democrats will continue to seem adrift, unfocused, united only by opposition, and without an identity that voters can perceive and be drawn to.

A political party of conviction will not seek to cobble together a set of unrelated appeals designed to create a fragile coalition. A party of conviction will state its core principles and invite all who share those principles to participate.

Neither party, Republican or Democratic, has a corner on the security of our nation. Neither party is more patriotic than the other, though political manipulators seek to make it seem so. With considerable justification it has been said that the first duty of government is to protect its citizens. In recent times Republican leaders have sought to underscore their "strength" by their more ready willingness to commit our armed forces, whether immediately justified by national security concerns or not, by widening the definition of national security to include regions and interests not normally associated with our security, and by spending more money on weapons.

Lacking their own clearly defined national security policy, Democrats have too often sought to insulate themselves from criticism by simply supporting these Republican initiatives. This is wrong. Even more, it is unnecessary. It is possible, indeed mandatory, for Democrats to fashion their own substantive security policy around principles of military reform and restructuring, prudent deployment of forces, much more dedicated support for the troops and their families in terms of accommodations, health care, and income, understanding of military history, and the formation of new security systems and alliances.

As the true costs of America's misadventure in the Middle East become apparent, the tasks of constructing a new national and international security policy and recapturing public confidence in our ability to provide secure borders will prove to be among the Democratic Party's greatest challenges. Meeting that challenge will first require a new understanding of the nature of security in the twenty-first century, then a more thorough appreciation for how the military must be reformed to respond to new threats and opportunities, and finally a sophisticated understanding of which challenges can be solved by military force and which cannot.

8

A NEW DEFINITION OF SECURITY

Security in the twenty-first century, both national and international, will be a vastly different enterprise than it was even in the late twentieth century. Its dimensions will include security of livelihood, security of community, security of the environment, security of energy, and security of our borders. Security of livelihood and the community are largely, though by no means exclusively, domestic and economic. Security of the environment and of energy are increasingly international concerns and require more creative national priorities. Security of our borders requires the defeat of radical Islamic jihadism and is the responsibility of a new and different military and intelligence community, but with increasingly integrated international cooperation.

As recently as the end of the Cold War, a mere decade

and a half ago, we were defining national security as the containment of communism and the prevention of a nuclear exchange. This definition seems quaint now. In the post–Cold War era, if I lose my job and the ability to provide for my family, I don't feel very secure. If my community loses its principal employer either to relocation or to foreign competition, those in my community are not feeling very secure. If my grandchildren's health is jeopardized by polluted air and water, their security is threatened. If local young men and women are recruited to fight in Gulf War III, IV, or V so that my neighbor can drive his Hummer, my nation is not secure. If the Homeland Security Department fails to meet its mandate to prepare for and respond to an attack, whether by al Qaeda or by Hurricane Katrina, my nation is manifestly not secure.

The Democrats have to redefine what security means in a world of globalization, climate change, dangerous energy dependency, and pandemic, and must offer new ways of addressing and reducing insecurity. Republicans wish to keep the definition of security narrow and traditional, as an effort principally of concern to the military. This is easier for them because they have traditionally not considered the Pentagon part of the detested "government," the same government that can produce the best military in the world but, in their mind, cannot do anything else well. Therefore, for Republicans the other facets of security are of only individual concern and can best be achieved through gated communities in naturally clean surroundings, private security forces, and the insulation from insecurity offered by private wealth.

The Republican outlook is certainly a plausible social attitude. It just happens not to be one that unites us as Americans.

Because the Democratic Party split asunder over Vietnam, a war whose central "domino" assumption turned out to be flawed, and has thereafter tended to oppose the use of military force as a first resort, we have been portrayed by Republicans as "weak on defense." This is an easy charge for those who see life as "nasty, brutish, and short" and who would just as soon punch someone in the nose as take the trouble to discover whether that person might have a legitimate grievance against us that might be satisfied without the sacrifice of American lives. But security has become more intricate, and simply punching someone in the nose or unilaterally invading his country may not achieve it.

No better illustration of this idea exists than Iraq. By unnecessarily invading Iraq, based on false assumptions, rather than relying on containment, the principle that won the Cold War, we will be living with the consequences for a long time to come. We should not go to war because we *want* to, but only because we *have* to. There was no imperative to invade Iraq.

Forget the convenient default justification of removing an evil dictator. We have never been in the evil-dictator-removal business. By our unprovoked invasion we have: created an international training camp for jihadists; released ancient Sunni-Shiite-Kurdish animosities; established the conditions for a restrictive theocracy where before a secular Arab society existed; increased instability in the most volatile region of the world; and, perhaps most of all, surfaced a Great White Whale to accommodate George W. Bush's latent Captain Ahab.

One would think that in the wake of the Iraq debacle, the Democratic Party's caution toward starting wars would seem statesmanlike to the American people, and it may well now. But this process was complicated by the massive mistake the party's leaders made in trusting the neoconservatives to set aside their long-held ambitions in the Middle East in the interest of authentic U.S. security. It proved to be a vastly misplaced trust. Rather than admit a mistake based on the systematic misleading by the Bush administration, Democratic leaders feel they have to "stay the course" to prove their "strength" on security matters. Thus does bad politics drive out good policy.

Democrats now are required to restate the fundamentals behind the constitutional balance of powers and the rights of citizens to be free of unnecessary government suspicion. This is the ancillary tragedy of Democratic support for the Iraq war resolution. Surely the Democrats in Congress who supported it could not have remembered how such sweeping congressional authorizations have been used by presidents in past times to justify unconstitutional actions at home. If nothing else, the Iraq war experience should stimulate serious insistence in America that Congress reclaim its constitutional authority and responsibility to declare war. Because of congressional cowardice, presidents now routinely trample on the Constitution and cow Congresses into acquiescence at the drop of a threat. The president may be commander in chief of the armed forces, but he does not possess the constitutional authority to commit this nation to war.

In the case of Iraq, much more plausible alternatives existed then and exist today, alternatives that did not require sacrifice of constitutional liberties. Those alternatives begin with a more comprehensive understanding of what genuine security is and how it can be achieved. What would follow are targeted policies to achieve security in this multifaceted security world. A new economic policy based on productivity (not consumption), the information revolution, a highly educated and trained workforce, and sustainable growth offers much greater security of livelihood than tax cuts for the rich. Such an economic foundation would make America's communities more secure by keeping our industries at home and employing American workers rather than relocating abroad and employing foreign workers.

A long-term program for energy security based on conservation, new technologies, and renewable sources would release the United States from dangerous reliance on Persian Gulf oil supplies, would liberate our foreign policy in the region, and would save thousands of American lives in multiple Gulf wars. Energy security as a central goal for the United States has the further security benefit of reducing insecurity from energy-related environmental pollution. Few experts outside the Bush administration argue that carbon-based energy consumption is unrelated to climate change and global warming. Rarely does a major change in a single but central domestic area, in this case energy consumption, offer such huge increases in our national security. Energy and environmental security must become a centerpiece of the Democratic Party's security platform.

The Democrats must also propose a new approach to the security of our nation's borders. Belatedly adopting only a few new approaches the military reform movement proposed twenty-five years ago, the Republican Party is attempting to "transform" our traditional combat forces to the previous century's style of warfare. Insufficient attention has been given to the greatly expanded special forces necessary to carry out the low-intensity urban conflict of the twenty-first century.

And the border protection and catastrophic response central to homeland security are disastrously insufficient. At the end of 2005, *more than four years after 9/11*, the 9/11 Commission found the U.S. government's homeland security efforts "disappointing" and "simply not acceptable." If this administration is so concerned with the war on terrorism that it would eavesdrop on its own citizens, how could it not take homeland security more seriously?

For one thing, it had ignored warnings of terrorist attacks to begin with. The U.S. Commission on National Security had strongly recommended the creation of a consolidated federal department, with a cabinet secretary accountable to the president, Congress, and the American people. But Vice President Cheney opposed the concept of a new department as a big-government mistake, and therefore no preparations were made to protect our borders or respond to attacks once they took place.

Meanwhile, Senate and House members, including many leading Democrats, decided in 2002 to move forward with a new department, but the White House did not want Democrats to get credit for homeland security. So, on a crash basis, administration officials cobbled together a department much more complex than that recommended by the Commission on National Security. Given its unnecessary and ill-planned complexity and presidential resistance to the new department in the first place, it was doomed to ineffectiveness.

None of this would matter, of course, if the security of American citizens were not at stake. It would take an epic hurricane, Katrina, to demonstrate what a hash had been made of homeland security. In effect, Katrina was the second "terrorist" attack, and four years almost to the day after 9/11, we failed. Even worse, administration officials knew they were unprepared: "Most of the world didn't see it [this hash] until Katrina," a senior administration official told the

Washington Post in December 2005, and so President Bush fiddled while New Orleans drowned, unable to accept or process bad news even from his compliant staff.

Taken together with the total failure—or even worse, the purposeful misconstruction—of intelligence before the invasion of Iraq and the equally total failure to plan for a potential insurgency and occupation, the dereliction of duty where homeland security is concerned borders on the criminal. For any administration to ignore warnings of terrorist attack, then resist organization of coordinated homeland security, then make a hash of it once forced to organize, is beyond incompetence. It is obtuse. It is willful ignorance. It is pure dereliction of duty. It deprives the president of any high ground or claim of "strength" where any genuine conflict with terrorism is concerned.

But as a party, rather than merely offering critiques from the sidelines, Democrats must present a comprehensive blueprint as to how this dire and dangerous situation is to be remedied, including legislative steps to prevent homeland security funds from continuing to be used as a wasteful, untargeted pork barrel for members of Congress.

Rarely in recent history has a Republican administration so weakened the nation's defenses that it opened the way for a comprehensive Democratic national defense strategy. Our conventional forces have been seriously depleted by repeated redeployments and by pathetically inadequate armor and equipment; our reserve forces, the National Guard and

Reserve, have also been degraded by redeployments and are not training and equipping for their vital homeland security mission. Our conventional forces are being "transformed" from traditional large armored divisions to smaller, lighter units, but the strategies for their use remain mired in traditional twentieth-century thinking; we need to expand the role of special forces. Both strategic and tactical intelligence are bogged down in yet another round of "reforms" that amount to little more than the shuffling of bureaucratic boxes. And most of the past four years has been wasted where border security, especially port security, is concerned.

Democrats must build their new vision of security upon an understanding that national security is no longer strictly a military concept. It now requires not only greater cooperation among democratic armies but also the integration of intelligence services and alliances to support failing states, to respond to mass migration, to prevent climate change, and to protect world oil supplies and distribution. The traditional concept of "national security" will soon give way to "international security," and it will be understood in this century as a much more comprehensive notion, one requiring superior military capability but also appreciating the limits of force in resolving many new sources of insecurity.

Where the military is concerned, efforts have been undertaken by the Department of Defense to restructure our military forces along the lines recommended twenty-five years ago by the military reform movement both in the Congress and among uniformed and civilian military experts. This effort, however, has been hampered by the ill-advised idea of Secretary of Defense Rumsfeld to prove his theories of lighter, swifter, more lethal forces in the invasion, and eventual occupation, of Iraq.

Because the possibility of prolonged occupation was never seriously considered, the restructured land forces, army and marines, have been severely overtaxed and undermanned in their new occupation capacity. Perhaps new, swifter, lighter U.S. forces can sweep away a third-rate army using theories of maneuver warfare. But that does not mean those same forces have the capability of occupying a country the size of California and suppressing widespread rebellion in a culture historically resistant to Western occupation.

Iraq should not be considered a fair test of the kind of forces required for the warfare of the future. Certainly low-intensity urban conflict characterizes that style of warfare, as we have learned at least twice in the city of Fallujah alone. But most needed in Iraq, following the overthrow of Saddam Hussein, were experts in nation building, civilian-military affairs, reconstruction, political system development, establishment of judicial systems, and a host of other specialties not included in the Rumsfeld reforms.

A Democratic defense program must emphasize both highly mobile special forces and nation builders, experts in reconstituting and restructuring failed states (especially those we have made to fail) and specialists in civilian-military affairs. If there are future Afghanistans, we will need, right behind our invading combat forces, those who can construct modern civil societies, specialists in economic reconstruction, agricultural, mining, and other experts, lawyers and judges, constitutional and legal teachers, and a host of specialties not normally associated with warfare. We are in far more danger today from failed and failing states than from ideologies and great armies in the field.

Today, and in the future, we will need a separate quasi-military capability, that of constabulary forces trained and equipped to maintain order while states are being rebuilt or gradually reorganized into new political entities.

In this age of failing and failed states, to a few of which we have contributed, as the very character of warfare is rapidly evolving, so too are the duties of the conqueror. Given the ultimate consequences of its eventual foreign and military policy in the Middle East, it was folly for President Bush and his administration to renounce nation building, for their policies have now put the United States into the nation-building business in a huge way. The problem is that we were not prepared for it. Once again, the Democratic Party is confronted with a challenge and an opportunity to add these duties to its long-range security policies.

The United States, led by the Democrats, must be much clearer concerning the conditions under which commitment of U.S. military forces should occur. Several seem obvious. First, a threat to our security must be immediate, verifiable, and unavoidable. Second, all diplomatic and political efforts to resolve conflict must have been exhausted. Third, the forces used must be sufficient to achieve our military and political objectives. Fourth, military forces should not be expected to resolve fundamentally political disputes. Fifth, the military objectives must be clearly understood prior to troop deployment. Sixth, all plausible scenarios should be studied and planned for. Seventh, there should be concurrence between civilian leadership and senior military commanders over the objectives to be achieved. Eighth, our political leadership should clearly state to the American people the costs and risks of the military operations and must obtain public support for the engagement, including possible long-term deployment of troops.

This kind of preamble to the use of U.S. military force has never been discussed, let alone adopted, by the Democratic Party.

Where the nation's security is concerned, politics must take a distant second place. The Democratic Party should not critique the misjudgments, mistakes, and historic blunders of the Bush administration simply for political advantage. But where the nation's security is at stake, an opposition political party would be derelict were it not to propose more plausible and effective alternatives to seriously flawed defense policies. What is unacceptable is unalloyed criticism; what is necessary is a better, more secure course. Though we have failed in this for at least twenty-five years, my party now has the opportunity and the obligation to design a comprehensive United States security policy for the twenty-first century.

9

LIBERTY AND SECURITY

For anyone with even a faint understanding of the pattern of conservative behavior in wartime, from the infamous Palmer raids after World War I through J. Edgar Hoover's excesses in the Vietnam era, it was as predictable as sunrise that the administration of George W. Bush would err on the side of extraconstitutional behavior in its conduct of the war on terrorism. The pattern is for presidents to obtain legal opinions from compliant White House counsel and an equally subservient attorney general assuring them that extraordinary circumstances justified extraordinary consolidation of power in the executive branch.

In this case, extraconstitutional behavior was further predictable because Vice President Cheney and Secretary of Defense Rumsfeld had vocally advocated more unilateral executive powers since the days of the Ford presidency in the 1970s, when excesses by the Nixon administration had led Congress to take its oversight responsibilities more seriously. Curiously, though, the Cheney-Rumsfeld theory of a powerful president seems to apply only when Republicans are in the White House.

The persistent argument seems to be that extraordinary times require setting aside the intricate balance of constitutional powers fashioned in 1789, if for no other reason than that James Madison and his fellow Founders could not possibly have understood the dangers represented by fascism, communism, terrorism, or whatever the threat of the day. This reasoning, of course, overlooks the profound historical fact that the Founders fashioned the Constitution with its unique checks and balances at a time when the incipient American republic was in the greatest danger of any in its long future existence.

Nevertheless, much wiser than we, the Founders clearly knew that the greatest danger came not from a long future list of "isms" but from a natural human tendency toward concentration of power. The constitutional distribution of powers, with checks and balances crafted like the finest Swiss watch, was to protect us from abuse of power not during times of ease but rather in times of crisis and peril.

Thus came revelations in late 2005 of presidential authorization of massive electronic and other surveillance of

American citizens by the National Security Agency over an almost four-year period, in clear violation of U.S. law. The United States government had also resorted to an unusual and undemocratic practice called "rendition," the summary kidnapping and forced transportation of suspects to torture-lenient countries where uncomfortable issues of due process and the rule of law could casually be swept aside. Then, of course, there was the systematic abuse of "detainees" by U.S. military and CIA personnel—"detainees" being an extralegal category, without the right of due process and other protections under our criminal justice system, or those of prisoners of war with rights under the Geneva Conventions.

Predictably also, we learned toward the end of 2005 that the FBI counterterrorism units had conducted surveillance and intelligence-gathering activities against a variety of groups having nothing to do with national security—groups concerned with the environment, animal cruelty, and poverty. And we may expect further revelations of a wide variety of excesses that will not become public until those responsible are well out of power.

All of this occurred, and predictably so, in the name of the "war on terrorism." We should have known that when criminal conduct by a stateless group was elevated to a "war," extraconstitutional behavior, violation of civil liberties, and abuse of power would occur in a variety of venues.

Indeed, it fit the plans of Cheney and Rumsfeld to declare war on a tactic, thereby enabling the long-sought concentration of powers in the president as commander in chief. It is doubtful in the extreme that they would have welcomed such concentration of power in a Democratic president. The Constitution, however, thank divine providence, knows no ideology or party.

Not knowing or studying their own history, many Americans seem stunned and amazed when presidents and their administrations abuse civil liberties in the name of security. Though by no means confined to one ideology, these abuses do seem the peculiar preserve of conservative Republicans who incline, in any case, more toward security, secrecy, and a "strong president," usually meaning one who can do whatever pleases him, than toward protection of free speech, of association, of the press, and of citizens' liberties.

Democrats, however, do not approach the subjects of constitutional rights and civil liberties with totally clean hands. Franklin Roosevelt, with the approbation of the U.S. Supreme Court, imprisoned tens of thousands of loyal Japanese Americans during World War II. Our government, rightly embarrassed by this mass violation of our own principles, later—much later—paid reparations by way of expiation. Harry Truman cut corners during the early years of the Cold War and during the Korean war, and John Kennedy, following the precedent of Dwight Eisenhower, gave our intelligence services enormous leeway in the form of Operation Mongoose, the effort to overthrow Fidel Castro. And Lyndon Johnson endorsed the infamous Phoenix program that targeted thousands of village Vietnamese, who may or may not have been guilty of collaboration with the Vietcong, for summary execution.

The issue is not whose hands are dirtiest. The issue is who has learned from this history of excess. In almost every case where liberty was sacrificed to obtain a measure of security, the sacrifice turned out to be unnecessary and ineffective. The Democratic Party should become, clearly and forcefully, the party of civil rights and civil liberties. If need be, it must confess its own past errors in order to gain public confidence. But it must state with clarity that constitutional liberties need not be sacrificed to ensure our security.

This means that unconstitutional excess condemned in one party cannot then be condoned when one's own party acquires power. Hypocrisy is a powerful force in human behavior. Actions that are frightening to us when carried out by those we oppose cannot then be acceptable when those we trust and support carry out those same activities. Where the U.S. Constitution is concerned, rights and liberties are ideologically blind. They stand above conservatism and liberalism. They are immune from party. Their erosion does not become acceptable simply because the party and leaders we favor are eroding them. If the Democrats are to become the party of civil liberties and protection of constitutional rights, we must take our stand even when it is a Democratic president or Congress undermining them.

It is often said that the first casualty of war is the truth. In fact, the first casualty of American war is the liberty of Americans.

Having served on a Senate committee that investigated and revealed similar abuses of power during the 1960s and '70s, I was not surprised that there would be a cyclical return to these patterns of abuse in the name of combating terrorism. Even for those with a proclaimed heritage of opposition to big-government power, there is an almost inevitable, reflexive concentration of power in the president and those closest to him in the White House whenever a threat, real or imagined, exists. It is ironic in the extreme, however, that those so busy with concentrating and abusing government power *after* 9/11 were so blind to the warnings of terrorist attack *before* 9/11.

Three weeks after I took the oath of office in the United States Senate, Majority Leader Mike Mansfield appointed me to the Senate Select Committee to Investigate the Activities of the U.S. Government. It soon came to be known as the Church Committee after its chairman, Senator Frank Church of Idaho.

The Senate had been moved to investigate the Central Intelligence Agency, the Federal Bureau of Investigation, the Defense Intelligence Agency, the National Security

Agency, and a host of other intelligence agencies by increasing reports of abuse of authority both by the agencies themselves and by previous administrations that had abused the agencies because of war fever. Throughout 1975 and much of 1976 the committee investigated these reports and issued recommendations to prevent future abuses.

During our investigations, we discovered widespread surveillance, wiretaps, and mail openings of a very large number of American citizens. The excuse given by the FBI and others for this program, code named Cointelpro, was, "We are at war and we need to do everything we can to defeat our enemy." Sound familiar?

The CIA conducted the infamous Phoenix program, which consisted of the systematic assassination of thousands of village Vietnamese accused of collaborating with the Vietcong. This was an earlier version of Abu Ghraib, with torture being replaced by "termination with extreme prejudice." During the Eisenhower and Kennedy administrations the United States also tried to assassinate at least six foreign leaders—in the case of Fidel Castro with almost fanatical insistence—but without success. Too bad we didn't have the Predator then. It would have been so much simpler. (The Predator is an unmanned, remotely piloted aircraft used for surveillance but also in some cases to fire precision munitions at suspected targets. Being a technological marvel, it is not required to concern itself with whether the target is a legitimate one.)

Many reforms were proposed and enacted in the wake of the Church Committee's findings. The Foreign Intelligence Surveillance Act of 1978 required special intelligence courts to approve national security wiretaps. The current Bush administration has found that statute inconvenient and, predictably, has ignored it. We recommended presidential "findings" before extraordinary covert operations were undertaken. This was not to undermine the CIA. It was to protect the CIA, which up to then had been left dangling in the wind when misused by presidents who wished to claim "plausible deniability" for operations that were discovered or did not turn out as planned.

That reform surfaced during another period of political abuse, the infamous Iran-Contra affair of the mid-1980s, involving Bible-shaped cakes, trading with the enemy, lying to Congress, and avoidance of accountability, when it turned out that Ronald Reagan, contrary to his own memory, had signed a "finding" authorizing the whole bizarre episode of trading arms for hostages held by Iranian-sponsored groups in Lebanon and then using the monies generated to fund the *contra* rebels in Nicaragua—all in violation of federal law.

Again to support the CIA, we laid the groundwork for the 1982 Intelligence Identities Protection Act that prevented identification of CIA operatives. This was the act violated by at least half of the Bush White House in its ideologically motivated efforts to punish one of its critics, Ambassador Joseph Wilson, by exposing his wife, who held an undercover position at the CIA—all because Wilson had disproved administration assertions that Iraq was obtaining nuclear materials from Niger.

Many defenders of President Bush said, "It doesn't matter. She had a desk job." They forget the history that gave rise to the Intelligence Identities Protection Act, particularly the "outing" of CIA station chief Richard Welsh in Athens, which in turn caused his assassination on Christmas Eve 1975. I know this because I was asked by the director of Central Intelligence, William Colby, to intervene with the White House chief of staff to obtain presidential approval to have Richard Welsh buried at Arlington National Cemetery. That chief of staff was one Richard Cheney.

So what goes around comes around. Here we are again, thirty years later, in yet another unwise war, no wiser and once again willing to sacrifice constitutional liberties in the name of security expediency. One has only to consider the behavior of the Bush administration during the Iraq war to appreciate how soon we forget, how little we learn, and how pervasive is the tendency to violate civil and constitutional liberties in the name of war. Virtually all of the reforms recommended by the Church Committee have been evaded, ignored, or violated in the name of the "war on terrorism." If there was one lesson all of us who served on the Church Committee learned, it was that there are no secrets, everything comes out, and the promises of improved security nearly always fail to justify the sacrifice of liberty.

If America is to prevail, it must grow up. We must learn from our mistakes, and not repeat them. We must finally understand that our security cannot be ensured by sacrifice of our own liberties. This is the leadership role advocated here for the Democratic Party: to teach this lesson.

If the Democratic Party is sincerely and effectively to be the party of civil liberties, it will be taking on a heavy burden. We are a pragmatic society and we expect results. If terrorists want to attack us, we expect our leaders to prevent it. We believe this protection can be provided under the same Constitution that also protects our rights and liberties. And in this belief we are basically correct. No instances come to mind where the suspension of checks and balances, setting aside the rule of law, or violation of the Fourth Amendment actually increased our security.

There is a very heavy burden on any American president who wishes to set aside these protections to prove his case. It would have helped if the Democratic Party, before many of its leaders gave open-ended approval to make war against Iraq, had been more cautious in considering its casual grant of authority to President Bush. Democrats could have done so by letting the American people know what kinds of con-

duct they were *not* approving in voting for the war resolution. But then, apparently too few Democrats in Congress
had a sufficiently vivid recollection of the excesses of Vietnam and Watergate or familiarity with their histories of
abuse of power in the name of security.

10

STEWARDS OF THE EARTH

Though none of the great Democratic presidents of the twentieth century can lay claim to being the "environmental president," in the 1960s John Kennedy (through his secretary of the interior, Stewart Udall) and Lyndon Johnson (through his wife, Lady Bird) dramatically raised public consciousness of the need for resource conservation, environmental protection, and the requirement that commercial development be sustainable.

As an early disciple of Rachel Carson, and influenced by her monumental 1962 book *Silent Spring*, Stewart Udall made conservation, soon to be called environmentalism, a central priority for the national government. Through his influence national laws requiring cleaner air and water and safer disposal of toxic wastes were drafted and eventually enacted, and these became the basic building blocks of the Environmental Age.

Once again, political irony surfaces. A century ago, concern for conservation was closely identified with a Republican president, Theodore Roosevelt. John Muir and other early preservationists led the effort to enlighten the American public to the threats to our natural heritage from rampant mining, timbering, railroading, and development, not only in the east but throughout the west. Even by the time I arrived in the U.S. Senate in 1975, there were still a few very strong Republican environmentalists, many of them from the northeast, like John Chafee of Rhode Island. They represented the increasingly diminishing elements of a great Republican preservationist tradition.

Those remaining heirs of Theodore Roosevelt were soon replaced by laissez-faire, antiregulatory, antienvironmental Republicans either unfamiliar with or totally opposed to their party's own rich traditions. The heavy lifting where natural resources conservation, wilderness preservation, and environmental protection were concerned fell by default to the Democratic Party, and we have borne it, with mixed success and uneven enthusiasm, ever since.

No serious person believes that economic opportunity, sustainably undertaken, is incompatible with environmental health and generational accountability. But that is the argument made by antigovernment, resource-plundering interests that have dominated the Republican Party for the past three or more decades. It is a bogus argument unsupported by the facts and one unworthy of a great political party and visionary leadership.

Resource stewardship is clearly related to the themes proposed for the Democratic Party's renaissance. There can be no *social justice* in a society where the young and the old are exposed to dangerous pollutants. Today, environmental concerns have clearly become global, through climate change, global warming, transnational migration of pollutants, ocean dumping, and a host of related international issues, all requiring *international alliance* for their remediation and prevention. Wise resource stewardship is also obviously a key consideration for those concerned with *civic duty* and citizen responsibility. And commercial practices that expose certain classes of citizens to unacceptable dangers clearly are incompatible with *equality and justice*.

Therefore, the Democratic Party must make stewardship of the earth a central guiding principle. Indeed, the party has little choice. The panoply of rising resource concerns are almost daily front page news. The party of corporate America, the Republicans, is not about to tighten regulations on polluters and pollutants. In fact, where dangerous elements such as mercury are concerned, the Bush administration has loosened restrictions on their indiscriminate dissemination. Where else are the people of America to go for protection if not to environmentally concerned Democrats?

Besides which, the most dramatic resource issue of the

century is carbon emissions from gas-combustion vehicles, particularly in energy-consuming (and energy-wasting) nations such as the United States. Carbon emissions are a rising global threat because they are a central cause of global warming. Our dependence on unstable foreign oil supplies is an even greater threat, for more immediate reasons. We have now fought two wars in the Persian Gulf region, one still under way, both having more to do with oil supplies than we, and our leaders, are willing to admit. Given our present policies and practices, we should fully expect to find ourselves fighting Gulf wars III, IV, and so on.

Dependence on foreign oil, the instability of its sources, the global impact of carbon emissions, the foreign policy implications of dependency on Persian Gulf supplies, the provocation that our oil greed offers for jihadists seeking recruits among alienated Muslim youth, and the not-so-subtle message we send the world—"that's *our* oil under their sand"—all these circumstances are at the center of the great American dilemma of the early twenty-first century.

Management of world oil supplies, production, distribution, and markets is, as much as terrorism and proliferation of weapons of mass destruction, the foremost challenge of our time. Indeed, this issue cannot be separated from the radical Islamic jihad against the United States and the vulnerability of intricate oil production and distribution systems to that jihad. If a Third World War occurs, it will be in the Persian Gulf and it will be over oil.

Most important, our unnecessary dependence on Persian Gulf oil supplies restricts our world leadership and undermines our moral authority. Literally no one in the world except self-deluded White House officials believes that our political, economic, and military interests in the Middle East have nothing to do with oil. Because we do not have the courage and integrity to admit that our true motives have much to do with oil addiction—and, given our profligacy, we have good cause not to—we appear The Great Hypocrite to the world at large.

We can, and do, spend billions of dollars trying to convince the world that we are engaged only in a high-minded attempt to bring the blessings of democracy to the Middle East and elsewhere. That may have the salutary effect of making American Hummer drivers feel virtuous. But it is laughable to think that the wretched of the Middle East or elsewhere are going to be taken in. And the oil (and oily) oligarchs who supply our addiction are laughing up their copious sleeves at us, even as they take tens of billions of our dollars to finance their great yachts, multiple mansions, swelling (and repressive) security forces, and, more to the point, protection money to al Qaeda to leave them alone.

We will be taken seriously as promoters of democracy only when we cure our petroleum addiction, release the hold the oil oligarchs have on us, take serious conservation steps, tax petroleum use and carbon production, drive efficient cars, and reclaim our national integrity. Then, and only then, can we arrive in the Middle East with clean hands and pure hearts, truly concerned with opportunity for the repressed Arab masses, democratic rights for women, freedom of speech for opposition parties, a free press, the creation of freely elected parliaments, representative government, and the rule of law. It is nothing but pure folly and self-delusion to think otherwise, to believe that we can fund repressive oligarchs with one hand while offering the promise of democracy with the other.

The poor of the earth are not mocked and neither are they ignorant. Poor people everywhere, including in the United States, may have slender means, but they are not stupid and they are rarely fooled, at least for long. They know—we know—what's up.

They know the Republican Party has an energy policy. It is this: We will continue to rely on foreign oil imports to fuel our energy-inefficient vehicles, and if those foreign supplies are cut off, we will sacrifice the lives of other people's sons and daughters to get the oil. Pretty simple. Pretty straightforward. Massively immoral.

The Democratic Party, on the other hand, has no coherent energy policy. It must develop one. It should be: We will make every effort to liberate the United States from foreign oil imports through conservation, increased fuel-efficiency standards for all vehicles, massive investment in next-generation vehicle propulsion systems, and carbon taxes. These steps represent a variety of approaches that must be synthesized into a comprehensive national program. The oft-cited commitment by John Kennedy to land a man on the moon is not an inappropriate analogy. As with other new approaches, what is lacking is not ideas and solutions, it is political leadership and will.

Beyond the national interest and what is best for America, and certainly beyond politics, resource stewardship is an ethical obligation. It is an intergenerational duty for one generation to seek to improve the lot of the next by turning over a world in better shape than it was found. Conservatives seem to consider legacy a purely private, individual consideration. All I have to do, they say, is look after my own children. I'll leave them a cozy nest egg, a private endowment, so they can find their own gated community on a pleasant hilltop with clean air and filtered water.

But nature cannot ultimately be privatized. Air and water belong to humanity. Water might be triple-filtered, but who wants to wear a nose mask? Carbon gases respect no guarded, gilded gates. Absent a radical restructuring of national priorities and restoration of national integrity, we can expect in the not-too-distant future that visionary developers will offer domed communities to those with great wealth on what is now wilderness land. But even so, we may run low on middle-income and lower-middle-income youth willing to sacrifice their lives so their wealthy neighbors can continue to drive their Hummers.

Even the humblest among us leaves a public legacy when

a private one cannot be afforded. That legacy is heavily weighted toward the condition of the earth and all that is on it. No generation has the right to plunder those resources. We are now at a stage in human development, in what should be enlightened evolution, where each generation must be held to account. The heyday of profligate squandering of nature and nature's bounty is over. The plunder party has ended. The bills for that party have now come due and must be paid.

We may wish to believe that this is not true, and we may persist in electing presidents and representatives who encourage us in our fantasies of endless exploitation, but nature possesses its own enduring and inescapable systems of justice and reckoning. The Democrats must have the courage and the conviction to say this. We must be the conscience of the nation on the issue of public legacy and generational accountability. To do otherwise is to sin against our own children. And for that sin, one can only pray there is a divine reckoning.

A principled position on stewardship of the earth is inevitably bound to anger certain corporate interests, especially those that carefully allocate their campaign contributions to Democrats and Republicans alike. Resource processing industries, chemical producers, pharmaceutical manufacturers, weapons developers, mineral extractors, and a host of similar interests spend billions of dollars lobbying against laws and regulations they consider restrictive. But they are the first to acknowledge that their sole obligation is a commercial one, the maximization of profits for themselves and their shareholders. Absent laws and regulations, society is dependent on corporate goodwill to protect it. The profit motive is an efficient engine of market economics. But the profit motive cannot identify the greater national interest.

Conservatives define the national interest as the sum total of all private interests (with the possible exception of national security, which they are forced to admit that market forces left to their own devices do not produce). But there is a separate, tangible, and identifiable national interest over and above the composite of special private interests. That national interest not only includes secure borders, it also includes a safe and secure environment. Where markets do not guarantee that, the people through their government are both entitled and obligated to do so.

This is a basic philosophical difference between conservatives and liberals: Are there or are there not national interests that only the people, through effective government, can secure?

Where our natural environment and heritage are concerned there is an added dimension. It is a spiritual one. We have not been put upon the earth, in our case on the rich North American continent, for the purpose of plunder and profit. We have a duty to respect and protect nature. In an age when the religious right has hijacked the domestic agenda, and in some ways also the foreign policy, of the

Republican Party, it is a source of amazement how little respect those elements have for the source of our material and even our spiritual well-being.

It has only been in very recent times that some members of the evangelical Protestant community have been heard to call attention to our obligations to our environmental birthright. These are welcome, if long overdue, voices. Whether the Democratic Party comes to make our stewardship of the earth a central principle, some of us as individuals will continue to do so. And we will continue to insist that our party, indeed both parties, and all Americans, restore some fundamental sense of the spiritual element embodied in the natural environment in which we live.

The issue of climate change is unavoidable. It is real and it is increasingly immediate. A prophetic NASA scientist, James Hansen, published this conclusion in late 2005:

> The Earth's climate is nearing, but has not passed, a tipping point beyond which it will be impossible to avoid climate change with far-ranging undesirable consequences. These include not only the loss of the Arctic as we know it, with all that implies for wildlife and indigenous peoples, but losses on a much vaster scale due to rising seas. . . . This grim scenario can be halted if the growth of greenhouse gas emissions is slowed in the first quarter of this century.

Within weeks thereafter, this prophetic voice was first censored and then censured by the Bush administration. In that same context, the writer and environmentalist Bill Mc-Kibben writes: "We are forced to face the fact that a century's carelessness is now melting away the world's storehouses of ice, a melting whose momentum may be nearing the irreversible. It's as if we were stripping the spectrum of a color, or eradicating one note from every octave. There are almost no words for such a change: it's no wonder that scientists have to struggle to get across the enormity of what is happening."

It is not too much to hope, even before irreversible climate change occurs, precious species are destroyed by the thousands, and the monumental polar bear sinks beneath the melting ice, that a political consensus might form in America, and in much of the rest of the world, that we will do our very best to protect, defend, and respect the God-given earth that nurtures and sustains us.

A truly great and historic political party would make this one of its central causes.

II

CITIZEN DUTY

Given the continuing resonance of John Kennedy's challenge that we take our duties as citizens seriously and give something back to our country, it is puzzling that Democratic presidents and leaders have not made more of the classic republican ideal of civic duty.

President Bill Clinton, using the model of City Year (a highly successful project founded in 1985 to engage young people in worthwhile community service), did follow through on Democratic initiatives from the 1980s to create Americorps, a national service corps, in 1993. Americorps has been, when adequately funded, effective at community improvement and has enriched the lives of the young people who have served in it. Predictably, however, Republican Congresses and presidents have marginalized Americorps and the idea of national service at every occasion. Funds have been reduced and less committed directors put in charge. The Democratic Party should revive Americorps and make it the symbol of citizen participation and civic duty.

Ancient Athens and republican Rome did not require a service corps or very much admonition toward citizen duty, for the Greeks and Romans understood civic virtue to be at the very heart of republican government. Though Americans salute the flag of the republic, few know why they do so or what the ideal of the republic represents. Given their animosity toward government, Republican Party leaders cannot be expected to extol the virtues of citizen participation in government. It is left to the Democrats to remind us why our founders created a republic and what its obligations and duties entail.

Perhaps it will require the entire nation to abandon the late-twentieth-century retreat into rampant individualism, autonomy, and animosity toward the federal government. This usually requires a national catastrophe. The brief period of national unity following 9/11 illustrates what can be done. It should not, however, require a catastrophe to demonstrate how dependent we all are on each other and how some national challenges require a united national response.

Our Founders knew that the very survival of the new republic required citizen participation in government, the exercise of the people's sovereignty, steadfast resistance to corruption of public systems by special interests, and a strong sense of the common good and the commonwealth. This is what Benjamin Franklin meant, in responding to the question of what form of government was being developed behind the closed doors of the constitutional convention, when he said, "A republic, if you can keep it."

This is by no means an unobtainable or unrealistic ideal. It does, however, require citizen commitment. Service on juries, attendance at public forums, service on community improvement committees, participation in elections, voting on every occasion, interrogation of public officials, monitoring city councils and state legislatures, self-education in the issues of the day, all are part of what citizenship in a republic requires. The problem, as Oscar Wilde summarized in his critique of socialism, is that it requires "too many evenings."

Despite the many personal concerns and obligations we all have, it is the duty of Democrats to maintain the central principle of republicanism: citizen duty and citizen responsibility. Without citizen involvement, sovereignty—power—shifts to those who make a concerted effort to achieve it. These are the special interests that spend billions on lobbying for their narrow concerns. Inevitably, this leads to the kind of cynicism and massive corruption of the public trust we witnessed, yet again, in the Washington of 2005 and 2006.

When citizens do not pay attention and decide not to be involved, they should not be surprised when the cancerous process of corruption sets in. And this process destroys the notion of the common good and the commonwealth. We all thus come to feel that we are in it for ourselves and not for our country.

These observations could be readily dismissed as unrealistic and idealistic were it not for the fact that they are at the very heart of republican society and government. The fact that many in power dismiss them as idealistic is a reflection of the degree to which we have sacrificed the essence of our form of government. All of the Republican Party's patriotic rhetoric cannot substitute for the real thing. Patriotism is not about slogans and clichés, flags in lapels or rampant behind the president on every occasion. It is about duty, participation, the sovereignty of the people, and commitment to the commonwealth. Absent these principles, the national interest is sacrificed and corruption of our public institutions is guaranteed.

It may be fine to suspect government power. It is not fine to use this as an excuse to neglect civic duty. Genuine conservatism suspects government even when its own representatives inhabit it. Today's conservatives think government power is fine so long as they are exercising, and occasionally abusing, it. Democrats may be guilty of the hypocrisy of abandoning their historic concern for justice and equality in an effort to move to the amorphous "center." But Republicans are surely guilty of the hypocrisy of opposing government only until they occupy it.

Can a mass democracy of three hundred million Americans also exercise classic republican virtues? I believe so.

Direct citizen participation in government, in addition to national service, can occur at the neighborhood and community levels. Thomas Jefferson thought he and his founding colleagues had made a mistake by not including in our original federal structures a political space in which every citizen could participate directly and immediately. But that does not mean we cannot create such a space for ourselves. Whether in Kittredge, Colorado (where I live), or in thousands of local and community governments across the nation, every citizen who cares to invest an evening or two can participate in the level of government that has the most immediate impact on his or her life.

The Democratic Party must recapture the Kennedy ideal, the ideal of ancient Greeks and Romans and those who have preferred their own sovereignty over that of the prince since the dawn of the notion of freedom. All Americans who proclaim their commitment to liberty and freedom, including conservative Americans, must back up that commitment with civic virtue, exercise of popular sovereignty, resistance to corruption, and proclamation of the commonwealth.

12

A NEW VISION FOR AMERICA

While wise and effective policies must be founded on immutable principles, they must also be relevant to the realities of the day. A domestic program based on justice, duty, and equality and a foreign policy based on international alliance in a global commons must relate to the new information economy, a precarious and costly health care system, energy dependence, climate change, mass immigration, massive trade deficits, astronomical private and public debt, homeland insecurity, proliferation of weapons of mass destruction, and a host of other new realities. In Chinese, the same symbol represents "danger" and "opportunity," and it is for the Democrats to use their foundation of restored principles to convert these dangers to new opportunities.

As the Republicans have shown in recent years, it is not

difficult to devise economic policies that benefit the rich. Simply cut their taxes and, if necessary and expedient, claim that this will stimulate growth. Whether cynical or simply unsound, however, this simplistic theory promises an economically and socially just society with opportunities for all—but only through the crumbs that fall from the overflowing tables of wealth.

A twenty-first-century Democratic agenda for social justice will include a recapitalized education base, with special emphasis on the sciences and technology; a safety net of health care for all; energy and environmental security; secure borders; and an economy based on investment and productivity rather than debt and consumption. These goals are not only necessary for national growth, opportunity, and security, they are also necessary to achieve a just society. All children, but poor children especially, require educational access and opportunity. All elderly, but particularly the elderly poor, require access to decent and humane health care. Our current energy dependence on foreign suppliers requires a military, disproportionately recruited from the working class, minorities, and the unemployed, to fight several more Gulf wars. The effects of a poisoned environment are almost always felt most immediately by those in poor neighborhoods, not those in gated communities. And those most burdened by debt and job losses attributed to factory flight are the unemployed and working poor.

It is a popular myth that when "the economy" is doing

well, everyone benefits. Take, for example, the issue of American children without health care. There was recently some fanfare that 350,000 children had been added to the rolls of the insured between 2000 and 2005. But this was not the result of actions taken by the United States government. It was the result of actions taken by several large state governments under the pressure of visible decline in the health of their children, many of whom lost health care coverage during the recession of 2002–2003.

Meanwhile, little notice was taken of the fact that during this same period, six million more Americans were added to the rolls of the uninsured, to bring the national total to forty-six million citizens without health care. On this issue, Governor Jennifer Granholm of Michigan told the *New York Times,* "Washington is utterly silent." By Washington, of course, she meant the Republican president and the Republican Congress. Democrats should make universal health care insurance for all Americans under age eighteen a national priority.

This agenda proposed for a Democratic renaissance is meant to restore America's foundations, not merely to benefit the poor and left-out. But it is also an agenda that is squarely in the Rooseveltian tradition, that will help close disparities in standards of livelihood, and that is founded on principles of justice. To make it, or something like it, the centerpiece of a twenty-first-century Democratic Party will remind the American people what the Democrats stand for and will draw sharp distinctions between us and a Republican Party clearly dedicated to concentrated wealth and power, laissez-faire economics, and devil-take-the-hindmost social attitudes.

Many Americans are rightly confused as to how the American economy can be said to be growing while they see very little evidence of it. In 2004, the national economy grew by 4.2 percent, the best gain since the boom of the 1990s. Yet at the same time, real median household income for households in the middle of the income curve (adjusted for inflation) fell for the fifth year in a row. And, as noted, with this the number of Americans without health insurance rose substantially.

How can this be? Because the economic growth was in the incomes of the most wealthy and among corporations. That is to say, the benefits of growth were not fairly distributed, and the infamous "trickle down" theories so favored by Republicans proved as false as they have always been. The so-called recovery beginning in 2001 saw corporate profits (once again inflation-adjusted) rise more than 50 percent while real wage and salary income rose by less than 7 percent.

At their best, particularly before the advent of "triangulation," Democrats always clearly and forthrightly stood for economic opportunity that benefited all Americans. It was left to the Republicans to foster fairy tales of "trickle down" and "supply side" mythologies to justify the luxury yachts and stupendous salaries of greed and wealth. Through minimum wages, collective bargaining, employment contracts, and a variety of middle-class and worker measures familiar to all advanced economies save, increasingly, ours, wealth can be spread and more broadly acquired. It is simply a question of courage and conviction.

One must have lived in America for close to seven decades to begin to learn the lesson of conservative perseverance. It is perhaps excusable for a young man raised in the late years of Roosevelt and challenged by the later age of Kennedy to believe progress to be permanent. That is to say, once we have struggled and achieved a new level of social and economic progress, it is here to stay. But that is seriously to underestimate the regressive gene in the conservative DNA. The lesson is: Nothing is final.

In late 2005, the Department of Justice operated by Alberto Gonzales on behalf of George W. Bush sought to reverse an important provision of the Voting Rights Act passed in the 1960s. Of course, like most Bush policies, this would not be done openly and honestly after full national debate. It would be done surreptitiously by its refusal to oppose a Georgia law requiring a $20 picture ID to vote. It took a federal court to strike down "what was little more than a modern-day version of the poll tax aimed at reducing turnout among poor minorities," in the words of a *New York Times* editorial.

That same Justice Department would overrule its own

career civil rights attorneys to approve the infamous scheme by House Majority Leader Tom DeLay to "illegally dilute the votes of blacks and Hispanics in order to ensure a Republican majority in the state's Congressional delegation"—again, quoting the *Times*. Those career attorneys who objected were ordered to be silent, and many were transferred out of their career commitment to civil rights into backwater jobs. So much for Republican "justice" and commitment to the Constitution. Restoration of constitutional government, to justice and equality for all, must be central to the restoration of the Democratic Party.

When all rhetorical debris is cleared away, we are left with a basic difference in outlook regarding the role of government. Republicans continue to believe that the least government is the best government, that most of its functions, save providing security (and that often through unconstitutional means), are malign, and that we are best off when we are left alone. Democrats, at least until recent years (when their knees became weak in the presence of the angry right), have seen government as an instrument of social progress, the means by which we demonstrate our humane instincts, and the force for regulating markets.

It is too extreme in both cases to say that all Republicans are against all government or that all Democrats think all government is good. But the respective philosophies are clearly in conflict and color virtually all attitudes toward the public agenda.

Political parties are most persuasive, and attractive, on those rare occasions when they become moral forces, when they rise above the competition for power and speak the truth. Such was clearly true for the Republican Party long ago in its abolitionist days and its progressive reform era. Such was also clearly true when Democratic leaders built a social safety net, rebuilt Europe and Asia after World War II, demanded civil rights and equal justice for all Americans, and reminded us of our civic duties.

To stand for the just, the right, and the good offers rewards far greater even than political power itself. Democrats should take hope from the knowledge that achieving power need not, except in times of corruption, require the sacrifice of principle, honor, and nobility.

The new century, with its new realities, now calls on the Democratic Party to apply the same intelligence, and hardearned moral authority, that it has demonstrated at the greatest periods in its past. Though mass south-north migration presents complex border protection issues, Democrats should stand for humane treatment of immigrants, and particularly their children, who are already here, at a time when demagogues are demonizing them. We can begin to address this complicated issue by revealing the hypocrisy of business owners who enrich themselves through cheap imported labor, and consumers who benefit from the cheaper goods, all the while demanding that our border with Mexico be sealed.

Further, the impact of climate change on future generations is as much a moral issue as it is an economic and environmental one. Democrats must frame this issue in those terms at a time when Republicans are cynically denying clear and preponderant scientific evidence.

Continued energy dependence, with its implicit reliance on military intervention and the sacrifice of American lives, has a moral component, and Democrats must make that case and be honest about the alternative sacrifices in conservation and cost required to save the lives of America's military.

Failed and failing states will threaten regional, even global, security. Democrats should advocate new international mechanisms for stabilizing fragile states to prevent ethnic and religious bloodshed.

The international arena offers the best opportunity to demonstrate an alternative vision to that of unilateral preemption. This is particularly true when our times in many ways parallel those of Harry Truman. His presidency occurred between the end of World War II and the onset of the Cold War. Today the Cold War is well over, but we have yet to introduce the idea of a new set of international structures to supplement if not replace those of the Truman era.

Belatedly, reforms of the United Nations are now under way. How effective they will be remains to be seen, but the Bush administration has demonstrated little if any leadership on the issue, preferring to criticize from the sidelines.

The American representative to the UN has done little more than obstruct real reform efforts and insist on "reforms" that all know have little if any chance of acceptance, all in the hope of further weakening the principal international organization dedicated to world understanding. It is a poorly kept secret that the Bush administration has nothing but contempt for this and other international institutions.

As a party, Democrats should have been heard from many months ago strongly advocating the importance of the United Nations, proposing its own thorough reforms, and proposing new missions for the organization that has made substantial contributions to the prevention of further world wars. But that voice was not heard.

Likewise, NATO, a Cold War institution, requires a new mission. The Democrats, as a party, should propose a new agenda for the premier Western security organization now that "containment of communism" is obsolete. But no agenda has been forthcoming.

The World Bank and International Monetary Fund should also be adapted to the new realities, including the economic impact of failing states and the need for massive increase in microlending. Currency stabilization through mechanisms such as Bretton Woods needs to be augmented by international banking and security regulatory agencies. New issues on the trade front require reform of the World Trade Organization and related institutions. But where are the Democrats?

The rise of tribalism, ethnic nationalism, and local conflict requires a new international peacemaking capability. At present, "peacekeepers" are defensively trained and equipped; they cannot make the peace where violence is occurring. The international community, led by the United States, must quickly construct a peacemaking capability that is offensively trained and equipped, that can suppress violence and conflict, and that can establish conditions sufficiently peaceful to permit diplomats to negotiate long-term political settlements. This is a powerful idea for Democrats to champion, especially in an age of Republican antialliance unilateralism. But so far the idea remains untouched.

The new century offers Democrats the opportunity to demonstrate the same vision shown by the Roosevelts, Trumans, Marshalls, Achesons, and others six decades ago. This cannot be done by individual Democrats offering piecemeal ideas for isolated problems. It requires the entire party and its leaders to unite behind a new international manifesto that demonstrates a clear understanding of the age in which we live, proves the narrowness and increasing irrelevance and ineffectiveness of the one-dimensional Republican view of the world, and places the United States once again at the forefront of the global community.

The great political issue of the twenty-first century will be national sovereignty and the ways in which we manage transition to a much more integrated world and international community faced with the necessity of addressing common problems in collective ways. Rules will change. Institutions will fade and new ones will be created to replace them. Nations will find themselves participating in new international structures, sometimes whether they want to or not, simply out of necessity, simply because they face challenges they cannot meet on their own. Even the Bush administration, willing to invade Iraq against international resistance, found it convenient to insist that Iraq was occupied by "coalition forces."

A new global vision for the Democrats will recognize the commonality of problems, the necessity of collective action, the imagination required to create new international institutions, the integration of markets, the interdependency of currencies and exchange, the shared interest in suppressing violence, the imperative to limit weapons of mass destruction, and a host of similar challenges to a shrinking planet.

If the Democrats fail to act, not only will the party suffer, but so will America, and so too will the rest of the world.

13

THE INDISPENSABLE POLITICAL PARTY

Few human institutions are indispensable, and fewer still deserve to be. Leaving aside institutions of enduring religious faiths, human institutions rarely last in historical terms, and few can claim indispensability for very long at all. But certain times do require certain institutions, including purely political ones, for certain specific purposes. Except to provide opposition to power, or to exercise power itself, there is neither constitutional nor historical necessity for a Democratic Party per se. By and large, political parties represent interests—constituent interests, special interests, sometimes very selfish interests.

To justify its existence beyond representation of interests, my party, perhaps all parties, must lay claim to popular loyalty and support by standing for and standing on principle.

Standing on principle always requires conviction, and in difficult times and times of unpopularity it sometimes requires courage. A party without conviction and unwilling to demonstrate courage can make no claim on citizen commitment and loyalty and may have no real claim to exist at all.

America is badly in need of a political party that will remind us of who we are as a nation by recapturing the definition given us by our Founders. We are not an empire. We do not seek territory. We have no ambition to rule the world. We will ally with others in the cause of democracy, but we will not seek to impose our will, our systems, or our beliefs on others. We are not crusaders. We claim no moral superiority to others. We recognize and respect cultures different from our own. We will exhibit goodwill to all until they give us cause not to. We seek neither foreign entanglements nor foreign demons to destroy. We will seek to prove the advantages of our political and economic systems by constantly trying to improve them and demonstrate, through those efforts, why these systems might prove beneficial to others.

For a student of America's founding era, all this is conventional wisdom, so much so that it would seem redundant to repeat it. But even a brief review of the conduct of our country since we abandoned the pursuit of al Qaeda in Afghanistan in favor of hegemony in the Middle East provides a sharp reminder of how far we have strayed from our founding principles as they have historically defined our nation's role in the world.

It will be argued that times have changed and that America's role must change with those times. That is true. But there is a vast difference between changing roles and changing character. The warnings and admonitions of our Founders had to do with America's maintaining its unique character in a world of clashing economic and political interests. They understood with ultimate pragmatism that we had to participate in that world, but they also understood with ultimate idealism that if we became as unprincipled as the nations of old we would lose our character and our unique contribution to the search for a better democratic republic founded on constitutional principles.

Even worse, as those in power try to make America into a nation it was not meant to be, they have resorted to the worst in our nature. In an age of cliché and bumper-sticker slogans used as substitutes for thought and ideal, Republicans have become masters. "Stay the course," "faith and values," "support the troops," all convey layers of meaning that cannot or will not be articulated. They make life easy for president and public alike. Democrats are not immune from superficial communications. We have our own code words and phrases: "the party of the people," "good jobs at good wages," and so forth. Even though the Republicans have shown themselves to be masters of the cliché, this is not to say that they are without principles. They believe in small government, low taxes, individual initiative, and risk taking on the high-wire of life, especially appealing to those born with their own safety net.

What is dangerous about the current neoconservative wing of the Republican Party is its purpose to use American military might to remake whole regions, regions like the Middle East, with ancient histories, complex cultures different from our own, religious differences, and resistance to Western hegemony. Often the best and most ideal causes are also those that change the nature of the people pursuing them. The road to hell, to resort to another cliché, is paved with good intentions. In this case it is not some kind of national hell we should be concerned with, but America's devolving into just another failed empire.

The Democratic Party has no choice but to become indispensable under these new conditions in this new age. It must become a necessary party, as it was during the Great Depression and at the dawn of the Cold War, a reminder of civic duty and citizen responsibility, and the party of equality and justice.

These are the principles our party should stand for and upon which it should build its policies in the early twenty-first century. Some in party leadership positions have wanted to play down the ideal of social justice and not assume any serious responsibility for those left out. This principle is a reminder of an age of liberalism, they say, and is unfashionable in today's political marketplace. Others seek to identify with the neoconservative unilateralist right in pursuit of its muscular policy of preventive invasion and occupation. Still others find the call to "give something back to your country" nostalgic and quaint. And many Democrats now have chosen to believe that racial justice and gender equality have been achieved, at least to the point that the American people will tolerate them, and that these subjects are best left alone.

When a political party abandons its long-standing principles, it has no choice but to find new ones if it means to be indispensable. It is not sufficient for the Democratic Party merely to fill the many vacuums left by the minimalist Republican dedication to individual autonomy. Nor is it sufficient merely to be what some have called the "nanny party," the authors of mazes of regulations and restrictions. Nor is it sufficient to be only caretakers of the poor, the neglected, the left behind, as urgent as many of those needs, produced by the more rampant versions of "trickle down" economic theories, are.

To become indispensable, the principles of the Democratic Party and the policies they produce must resonate with a cross section of Americans, they must be relevant to the current age of revolutions, and they must offer hope of a better nation. Deep in the soul of many if not all Americans is the notion that we can still do better, that we have not yet achieved our destiny, that there is still more to be done to "form a more perfect Union." This search for nobility, for it is nothing less than that, may be unique among nations. It is certainly rare, and it does not always characterize the American imagination.

But when we unite, usually in times of desperation, need, threat, or attack, we sense a higher goal than mere personal wealth and aggrandizement. Distinctions of class and wealth recede, selfishness and self-interest are placed aside, at least for the moment, and the common good and national interest emerge. I have always felt that concern for children represented a powerful common human thread. That accounts in large part for my singular preoccupation with intergeneration accountability and commitment.

As we have used concepts such as containment of communism and war on terrorism as central organizing principles of our society and nation, why could we not now use the ideal of a better nation for future generations as our society's central organizing principle?

If we were to do so, it would completely revolutionize our social policies. We would be more careful about unprovoked military invasions. We would pay much more attention to the preservation of clean air, water, and land. We would naturally wish to preserve species so that our grandchildren might see them as we have. We would set aside public resources, minerals, timber, wetlands, wildlife preserves for future enjoyment. We would conserve valuable energy supplies. We would protect recreation areas and parks. We would build museums and libraries as monuments to history and learning rather than build twenty-thousand-square-foot private mansions as monuments to private greed, consumption, and ego.

No single political party can achieve this kind of revolution in national values and priorities all at once. But it is not a bad place from which to start the renaissance of the Democratic Party. "Our children's future" as a unifying theme is not incompatible with "containment of communism" or "war on terrorism." Indeed, it ensures that we do not sacrifice the better angels of our nature and our humanity as we battle various forces of evil.

If we can unite the nation against evil, why can we not unite the nation for good? Why can we not dedicate ourselves, our lives, our fortunes, and our sacred honor to the cause of a better nation and world to be left to our progeny?

Surely there is evil in the world. We may differ over whether divine providence has commissioned the United States of America as its avenging angel to rid the world of that evil. But there can be little difference over concern for our children. This is one of mankind's most basic instincts. Indeed, this instinctive sense is one we share with the birds of the air and the beasts of the field. We care for our young. We consider those who do not do so as lower than barbarians and not worthy of inclusion in civilized society. Care for our young is one of the most powerful qualities of civilization itself.

My party would do well to restore this theme to the center of our national agenda. It transcends class, race, region, ideology, and religion. It is a powerful force for unity. The principal political difference between the two political parties occurs over the question of whether concern for our children is merely a private concern or also a public concern. Certainly wealth and status offer much greater hope of comfort for the future generations whom Fortune has chosen to inherit it. But that, alas, does not encompass the vast majority of us. And yet we are all custodians of a public legacy that not even the greatest wealth in the world can guarantee. That public legacy of nature in good health, a nation and a world at peace, a fair share for all, opportunity for those able to accept it, a tiny planet successfully navigating through the vast universe, all require a unified nation and society and increasingly a unified world and society.

To justify its existence on a plane above power and politics, a party must possess a soul. If it does not, it is no more than a transient vehicle for personal ambition and the service of special interests in the never-ending and ever-elusive search for power. A political party without a soul inspires no youth, dreams no dream, lifts no heart, offers no hope, ignites no inspiration, challenges no imagination, provides no promise of a better future.

What good is such a thing? Why support it? Why dedicate great portions of one's life to it? Why work for its candidates for office? Why give it money? Why bring others to its cause? Why place personal concerns aside in its mission? Why care at all?

Too often in the recent past, we have succumbed to the temptation of believing that more money, more slogans, more evasion of confrontation, more sophisticated media advisers, more access to television, more courtship of lobbyists and interest groups would satisfy the emptiness in our souls.

It was never to be. There is no political salvation down that path. All the money in the world, the cleverest media manipulators, the pollsters and focus-group experts cannot provide one thing: the soul of a party. A party, like an individual, must look within itself for its principles, for where it will draw its lines, for the boundaries of what it will and will not do.

There simply is no technical or financial fix for lack of purpose and direction. Without the compass of principle, the party and its candidates will be pulled in a thousand incompatible and largely irrelevant directions in search of acceptance. There is no political analyst or adviser in the world who can provide a candidate's principles.

There is no shortcut to conviction or to courage.

The Democratic Party must once again become the indispensable party. It must be the instrument for social change, for the preservation of our natural heritage, for equality for our many races, for opportunity for those who work, for the prudent use of military force, for protection of our borders, for resurrection of community, for equal justice for all, for hope that the future can be better, for concern for future generations. And it must do so because of its historic principles and beliefs and not merely its ambitions for power.

Principle is incompatible with calculation. Principle is steadfast and unchanging. Principle does not yield to expediency. Principle does not lend itself to personal ambition alone. Principle requires certain behavior and rejects other behavior incompatible with it. Principle conditions policy and sets its boundaries. Principle is a rock and a foundation. Principle abides even in an unprincipled age. Principle is a compass. Principle cannot be manipulated, compromised, or traded.

The Democratic Party must experience a restoration of its historic principles—*social justice, international alliance, civic duty, equality and justice*. This does not guarantee political success. It does guarantee purpose, dignity, and honor. It guarantees a party upon which the American people can depend. The restoration of Democratic principles will offer a beacon and promise to the nation. There is no guarantee that the nation will follow the beacon or accept the promise. America has deviated from principle before, and, sadly, it will do so again.

But when America strays, the Democratic Party will be there to call it home to its better nature. When America experiences a long-overdue concern for the poor, we will be there. When Americans realize our present foreign policy is leading us into isolation from our friends and allies, we will be there to reenter the community of nations. When Americans have a revival of the conservation of nature, we will be there. When a new generation of immigrants seeks democratic asylum, we will be there to welcome them. When our countrymen broaden their understanding of the true nature of security, we will be there to help achieve it. When any race or nationality on our shores is reviled and threatened, we will be there demanding justice. When an elderly woman is alone and without proper medical care, we will be there. When a child is neglected, we will be there. When young people lack purpose and direction, we will be there to challenge them to serve their country.

We will do these things and more for one simple reason: Our principles require it. We cannot do otherwise. We must know who we are and we must be who we must be. We must have principles. We must set our principles high. And we must always strive to live up to them.

When we have done so, when we have had a restoration of the Democratic Party's historic principles, we will have become indispensable to our nation. We will have elevated ourselves above mere politics. We will have the respect of Americans because we will have earned it. Even when out of power, even when our beliefs are not in favor for the time, we will have our purpose, our dignity, and our honor.

We will truly have become indispensable. We will have recaptured our convictions. We will have regained our courage.

We have no other choice.

A TWENTY-FIRST-CENTURY
DEMOCRATIC MANIFESTO

We, the Democratic Party, believe in:

- A national community based on social justice and equality for all;
- Restoring popular sovereignty and civic duty in the American republic;
- New international alliances to respond to the challenges of our time.

These principles of our platform reflect the values of our greatest presidents. Franklin Roosevelt united our nation into one community by establishing the Four Freedoms and the commitment of our society that no American be left behind. Harry Truman created a set of international structures to restore democracy after World War II and to defeat communism. John Kennedy restored the ideal of civic duty and service to our nation. Lyndon Johnson demanded equality for all our citizens.

We are living in a revolutionary age. Rigid ideology, right or left, will not suffice. Globalization, information, failed states, and the changing nature of conflict are the revolutions we face. Our new realities are proliferation of weapons of mass destruction, mass south-north migration, climate change, viral pandemics such as AIDS and avian flu, international markets and finance, eroding nation-state sovereignty, and a host of other challenges requiring a new international order mirroring the one created in 1946–47.

Only the Democratic Party can respond to these revolutionary new realities because it alone believes in social justice and equality, in the sovereignty of the people, and in an internationalist foreign policy.

These are our convictions. And we know it will require courage to be true to them.

A NOTE ON SOURCES

Since this is a work of political exhortation, it naturally draws on a lifetime of thinking, writing, and reading on related subjects. Some of the material in this book builds on arguments that I have published elsewhere, or that have been published by others, and in this note on sources I provide an accounting of these works. Except when otherwise noted, the sources cited here are the work of the author.

The quotation on page 22 is from Francis Fukuyama, "After Neoconservatism," *New York Times Magazine*, February 19, 2006.

On pages 24–25, the letter from a group of legal scholars urging the Senate to affirm the rights of Guantánamo prisoners to challenge their detention was cited in Eric Schmitt, "Democrats Provided Edge on Detainee Vote," *New York Times*, November 12, 2005.

The discussion on pages 28–29 of the unwillingness of those in power and those who support them to acknowledge the disturbing realities and troubling consequences of the war in Iraq builds on the author's opinion piece, "Who Will Say 'No More'?" *Washington Post*, August 24, 2005.

The analysis of the state of American liberalism circa 1972 on page 33 quotes from *Right from the Start: A Chronicle of the McGovern Campaign* (New York: Quadrangle Books, 1973), p. 328.

The works cited on page 42 are George Crile, *Charlie Wilson's War: The Extraordinary Story of the Largest Covert Operation in History* (New York: Atlantic Monthly Press, 2003), and Steve Coll, *Ghost Wars: The Secret History of the CIA, Afghanistan, and Bin Laden, from the Soviet Invasion to September 10, 2001* (New York: Penguin Press, 2004).

The work by John Lewis Gaddis cited on page 48 is *Surprise, Security, and the American Experience* (Cambridge, Mass.: Harvard University Press, 2004).

The discussion on page 89 of the limits of the neoconservative vision of a semipermanent, Korea-like stabilizing force in Iraq is an expansion of an argument first made in "And Now for Their Next Trick . . . ," *Financial Times,* January 4, 2006.

The analysis of the balance between pragmatism and moral leadership in American foreign policy, on page 103, is excerpted from Daniel Yankelovich, "Poll Positions," *Foreign Affairs,* September/October 2005, p. 10.

A more thorough treatment of the "new definition of security" for the twenty-first century, discussed in chapter 8, can be found in *The Shield and the Cloak: The Security of the Commons* (New York: Oxford University Press, 2006). The quote from a "senior administration official" about Hurricane Katrina is from Susan B. Glasser and Michael Grunwald, "Homeland Security Agency Is Victim of Bureaucratic Warfare," *Washington Post,* December 22, 2005.

On pages 136–37, regarding a set of standards to govern the commitment of American military forces, see also the author's lectures, "Enlightened Engagement," delivered at Georgetown University in July 1986.

The brief history of compromised civil liberties in the name of national security offered on pages 147–48 builds on "Intelligence Abuse Déjà Vu," *Los Angeles Times,* December 21, 2005.

The quotation on page 159 from NASA scientist James Hansen is from a presentation to the American Geophysical Union, as quoted in *The New York Review of Books*, January 12, 2006. The statement by Bill McKibben that immediately follows is drawn from the same *New York Review* article.

The discussion of the Jeffersonian ideal of citizen service in chapter 11 builds on *Restoration of the Republic: The Jeffersonian Ideal in 21st-Century America* (New York: Oxford University Press, 2002).

The statement by Governor Jennifer Granholm of Michigan on page 168 was quoted in John M. Broder, "Health Coverage of Young Widens with States' Aid," *New York Times*, December 4, 2005.

The discussion of the false economic recovery on page 169 draws on data from Paul Krugman, "The Joyless Economy," *New York Times*, December 5, 2005.

On pages 170–71, the quotations from the *New York Times* editorial concerning the Georgia law requiring a $20 picture ID to vote are from "Fixing the Game," December 5, 2005.

ACKNOWLEDGMENTS

Whatever credit this book might enjoy belongs principally to Paul Golob, my extraordinarily capable and professional editor and friend. In August 2005, the *Washington Post* published an impassioned—some might say inflammatory—opinion piece that I had entitled "Waist Deep in the Big Muddy" but which the *Post*'s headline writer thought might be more appealingly entitled "Who Will Say 'No More'?"

The argument of the piece was that leaders of the Democratic Party had seriously erred in trusting the George W. Bush administration's representations concerning the danger Iraq represented to U.S. national security and, sotto voce, the relative ease of deposing Saddam Hussein and making Iraq a haven for U.S. influence in the troubled Middle East.

Acknowledgments

Given the way things have turned out there, virtually standing the administration's arguments on their head, it seemed to me reasonable that Democratic leaders (if not also some thoughtful Republicans) might now want to recant, chastise the Bush administration for misrepresentation, and propose a workable exit strategy, after two and a half years of unprofitable occupation.

The piece caused some controversy, and within a matter of weeks a number of Democratic leaders did in fact confess error and announce their opposition to our occupation, though this was, given present tragic circumstances, bound to happen with or without the reference to the "Big Muddy" of the Vietnam era.

In any case, Paul's sensitive publishing ear picked up some resonance of the piece and proposed this book. The Democratic Party's dilemma extends well beyond the Iraq war. I have argued here that Iraq is merely a symptom of what happens when a political party finds itself adrift, rudderless, dismasted, with no one at the helm. Though criticism of one's own political party, after some four decades of service in the interest of its historic principles, does not come easily, sometimes duty requires one public servant's view of the truth to be told.

In addition to Paul, finally, I owe an unpayable debt of gratitude to the truly great members of the Senate with whom it was my honor to serve.

INDEX

Index

Index

ABOUT THE AUTHOR

GARY HART represented Colorado in the U.S. Senate from 1975 to 1987. He is the author of seventeen books, including *The Shield and the Cloak* and *Restoration of the Republic*. Hart has lectured at Yale, the University of California, and Oxford, where he earned a doctor of philosophy degree in politics. A lifelong Democratic reformer, he is currently a professor at the University of Colorado, a distinguished fellow at the New America Foundation, and chairman of the American Security Project. He resides with his family in Kittredge, Colorado.

Printed in the USA
CPSIA information can be obtained
at www.ICGtesting.com
LVHW091133150724
785511LV00001B/107